dreds of books purporting to tell you how to get to the
tt Addis takes you far beyond that. In *Summit*, you will
ways to reach your own personal Everest . . . to transform
oy a richer and more rewarding work life and personal life."

—Dennis Pillsbury, Associate Editor, *Rough Notes* magazine

s takes the concept of improving oneself and turns it into a
tegy in *Summit*. The result is not only an innovative approach
ng individual success, it's also a powerful path toward real and
omer satisfaction."

—Michael Port, *New York Times* bestselling author
of *Book Yourself Solid Illustrated*

mit, winning CEO Scott Addis shares lessons about personal
and leadership he has gleaned from a lifetime of active learning.
re interested in bringing the best out of yourself and those around
u will benefit from the strategies found in this highly readable book."

—Bernard Dagenais, President and CEO,
The Main Line Chamber of Commerce

ust-read for every aspiring entrepreneur and experienced executive.
mit provides wise insights and original framework for success learned
he business world but necessary to living a good life. Scott Addis comes uncommon sense with keen business acumen in a book that will
lp better serve your customer and yourself."

—Joseph T. Cox, Ph.D., The Haverford School

I view *Summit* not only as a terrific independent resource but also as
especially valuable to anyone involved in Scott Addis programs. For
those readers, it will serve to notch up their participation and traction for
assignments and sessions. *Summit* is an insightful and motivating read!"

—Bill Harwood, Cofounder and Managing Partner, New Level Partners

"*Summit* is a must-read primer for aspirants and a refresher for seasoned
business professionals."

—Richard J. Anthony, Sr., Founder, The Entrepreneurs Network

"Scott's book is full of wisdom and insight for career success. Getting to
the summit should be everyone's aim to experience self-actualization."

—Peter A. Arthur-Smith, Founding Principal, Leadership Solutions, Inc.

# PRAIS

REACH YOUR PEAK
AND ELEVATE YOUR
CUSTOMERS' EXPERIENCE

# SUMMIT

## F. SCOTT ADDIS, CPCU, CRA

GREENLEAF
BOOK GROUP PRESS

Published by Greenleaf Book Group Press
Austin, Texas
www.gbgpress.com

Distributed by Greenleaf Book Group LLC

For ordering information or special discounts for bulk purchases, please contact Greenleaf Book Group LLC at PO Box 91869, Austin, TX 78709, 512.891.6100.

Design and composition by Greenleaf Book Group LLC
Cover design by Greenleaf Book Group LLC

Cataloging-in-Publication data

Addis, F. Scott.
   Summit : reach your peak and elevate your customers' experience / F. Scott Addis.
—1st ed.
   p. : ill. ; cm.
   Issued also as an ebook.
   ISBN: 978-1-62634-041-1
   1. Success in business. 2. Self-realization. 3. Customer relations. I. Title. II. Title: Reach your peak and elevate your customers' experience

HF5386 .A33 2014
650.1                                        2013945040

Part of the Tree Neutral® program, which offsets the number of trees consumed in the production and printing of this book by taking proactive steps, such as planting trees in direct proportion to the number of trees used: www.treeneutral.com

TreeNeutral®

Printed in the United States of America on acid-free paper

14 15 16 17 18 19   10 9 8 7 6 5 4 3 2 1

First Edition

*To Bobbie, Andrew, Jeff, and Will. It is because of you that my life's journey has been so fulfilling. You are my climbing team.*

# CONTENTS

Over the years, various publications have asked me to contribute articles on the trials and tribulations of the industry in which I have built my career—insurance and risk management. Although I have achieved success, I bear scars and wounds in evidence of the challenges and dangers that come with one's quest to reach the peak. Consequently, the articles I have written span a wide range of topics that extend far beyond the concerns of my profession. In studying these pieces, I saw that those topics fit within the framework of reaching one's peak and thus were applicable to almost anyone at any point in his or her life journey.

The idea of reaching your peak centers on disciplines and skills that support achieving your full potential to maximize performance. The peak represents the point where potential and superior performance intersect.

When it came to putting the material into a book, I thought it seemed natural to organize and edit the writings into a sequence that reflected a progression from individual skill development to business relationships to the customer experience. *Summit* is therefore divided into four elevations:

### Elevation I:
Preparing for the Climb (Developing Your Personal Readiness)

### Elevation II:
Setting Up Base Camp (Preparing to Present Yourself to Others)

### Elevation III:
On to the Summit (Focusing on the Customer Experience)

### Elevation IV:
The Final Ascent (Discovering Your Inner Strengths)

The last few steps of the climb are the toughest yet the most rewarding. They will require mental toughness, commitment, drive, self-discipline, positive attitude, and positive self-image. And it is when you make your final ascent that you will discover your inner strengths.

Whether you are starting out in your career or are an experienced business professional, I hope that you will find something in these pages to support and strengthen your efforts to achieve your full potential—to take you straight to the peak to benefit yourself, your family, and your customers.

# The Purpose of Your Climb

*Live your life each day as you would climb a mountain. An occasional glance towards the summit keeps the goal in mind, but many beautiful scenes are to be observed from each new vantage point. Climb slowly, steadily, enjoying each passing moment; and the view from the summit will serve as a fitting climax for the journey.*
**—Harold V. Melchert**

*S*ummit: Reach Your Peak and Elevate Your Customers' Experi-*ence* is for talented people like you who need both a nudge and a dose of confidence to begin your transformational journey—to get started, to leave ordinary behind, to move beyond the status quo. To make a difference in a world that so desperately needs difference makers. To elevate your personal performance with the goal of delivering a memorable customer experience journey!

Are you looking for a route to follow to help you realize your potential, a path along which you capitalize upon your natural strengths and Unique Abilities® and thus are able to reach your goals, dreams, and aspirations? If so, I have a hunch that the concept of *transformation* resonates with you.

"Transformation" is an intriguing word with a deep meaning: to be transformed, to change outer appearance and inner character; to become better, more than you are today; to open up possibilities for your future success. In other words, it could be defined simply as reaching your peak.

Your potential, what you are capable of becoming, represents your capacity for growth and development. Does your performance reflect your potential? If the answer is no (and I bet it is), *Summit* will reveal tools, strategies, systems, and exercises to assist you in maximizing your capabilities. This book will help you close the gap between your potential and your performance. It will give you clarity, purpose, and passion.

As you were growing up, you experienced peak performance on many occasions. It might have been the goal you scored in a soccer game or the amazing performance you gave in the school play. Perhaps it was the A+ you received on the paper you worked so hard on or the feeling you got when your parents beamed with pride as you accepted your high school diploma. Remember how you felt after each of those moments of peak performance—the exhilaration, the confidence, the energy? Has it been years since you experienced that tingly feeling?

Most people dream of a more fulfilling life, yet their circumstances and complexities of life get in the way of their journey to the peak. It is becoming a sad commentary on our society that most of us have lost sight of the beauty of the summit, the rewards of fully realizing our potential. If you think your plans, goals, and dreams may have fallen into someone else's hands, and if this has been affecting your ability to build and maintain business relationships and serve your customers' needs, *Summit* is written for you.

Paul Stoltz, the originator of the Adversity Quotient (AQ) and PEAK Learning (www.peaklearning.com), is the foremost expert on human resilience, the ability to endure setbacks yet progress to the next level of success. An avid mountain climber, he believes each of us fits into one of three types: (1) quitters, (2) campers, and (3) climbers.

Quitters find reasons why something can't work. They are often bitter, resentful, and the loudest whiners. They retired twenty years ago but never told anyone. They tell stories about how great they once were, but something has taken its toll and now they define themselves as victims.

Campers, on the other hand, have worked very hard to find a safe plateau in life. They admit that they have been aiming for a particular spot all of their lives and now they have reached it and are content to just camp there. Stoltz's research indicates that 80 percent of today's business professionals are campers, and many managers are simply campground leaders who likewise have settled into a safe, shady spot on their career path. At some point on their journey, the toll became so great that they stopped climbing and sacrificed their dreams, goals, and aspirations.

The good news is that inside every camper is a climber. Climbers never stop learning and growing. They are relentless in their pursuit of their goals in life. They inspire us because they see future potential. They have purpose and passion in everything they do.

If you are a camper or a climber, *Summit* will offer you an exhilarating journey to discover the highest reward—your potential! You can read in the order presented, but individual chapters are also freestanding and can be read at random, depending on your interests and needs. I am confident the ideas I share with you will apply to your career and your business wherever you are on your path to peak performance.

Growing up in a suburb of Philadelphia under the watchful eye of my grandfather, J. Fred Vollmer, I was taught—among other lessons—the importance of hard work, the value of relationships, and the impact of first impressions. A young man of modest means from south Philadelphia, Freddie (as he was known to me) went on to become the president of the National Restaurant Association in 1953. He was my mentor and best friend until his death at age seventy-five in 1977. And he remains my inspiration and my rock.

An All-American soccer player at the University of Pennsylvania, Freddie often used an expression most people have never heard: "present your card." The words originally came from Freddie's college coach. To him, the act of presenting your card was a public declaration, a message representing a state of being ready, fully prepared—physically, mentally, and spiritually—to perform at your highest level. For my grandfather, presenting his card let the competition know the serious nature of his game; presenting his card made the opponent aware that he would give it his best, try his hardest, and *never, ever* give up. Freddie used those words to challenge and motivate me before important events, including tests, exams, and athletic contests. Here is one such time I will never forget.

The date was November 1, 1975. I was a sophomore on the Princeton University soccer team and had been told by my coach that I would cover Steve Ralbovsky, the 1975 Hermann Trophy winner (soccer's equivalent of the Heisman Trophy). He was the star of Brown University, the number one ranked team in the United States. It was a foregone conclusion that Brown would easily win the game, as Princeton had been the doormat of the Ivy League for the previous few years.

Just before kickoff, Freddie signaled me to come to the side-lines. He looked me squarely in the eyes, and from deep inside his heart and soul he said, "Scotty, I just have three words for you—*present your card.*"

Within the first minute of the game, I unleashed a fierce tackle on Ralbovsky. I let him know that I would not be intimidated. As he got up off the ground, he could see the look in my eyes. He knew that he was in the battle of his life. For the remainder of the match, I never left his side. By the time the game ended, the score Princeton 2, Brown 1, Steve Ralbovsky was a beaten man.

As the years have passed, I have come to understand that presenting your card is about performing at your highest level—in your life, your business, and your community. The expression has less to do with winning versus losing and more to do with the *qualities of character* you bring to your game. It is about courage, commitment, focus, passion, positive attitude, problem solving, integrity, trustworthiness, self-discipline, selflessness, respectful-ness, generosity, and teamwork.

When confronted with a challenging project or task, I suggest that you ask yourself if you are prepared to present your card, if you are ready to give it your all, your best. In my book, presenting your card is a requirement if you are to climb to the peak. As Olympian Wilma Rudolph put it so exquisitely, "Never underestimate the power of dreams and the influence of the human spirit. We are all the same in this notion. The potential for greatness lives within each of us."

# Preparing for the Climb (Developing Your Personal Readiness)

*One cannot climb at all unless he has sufficient urge to do so. Danger must be met (indeed, it must be used) to an extent beyond that incurred in normal life. That is one reason men climb; for only in response to challenge does one man become his best.*

**—Ax Nelson**

You don't have to be an experienced mountaineer to know that you can't just wake up one morning and decide to climb a big mountain that day. Such a major undertaking requires careful thought, planning, and preparation—not to mention packing.

Similarly, the challenge of reaching peak performance is not something to take lightly or to enter into carelessly. You need to pay attention to four performance indicators and develop them actively: (1) your natural strengths, (2) your passions and interests, (3) your vision and goals for the future, and (4) your work-life balance.

In the next four chapters I explore these aspects of planning and preparing to ascend the summit, and I will show you how these steps are essential to your self-development, your career, and your business success.

# CHAPTER 1

# Assessing Your Natural Strengths

*The potential of the average person is like a huge ocean unsailed,
a new continent unexplored, a world of possibilities waiting to be
released and channeled toward some great good.*

**—Brian Tracy**

A number of years ago I had the good fortune of being introduced to Dan Sullivan, founder and president of Strategic Coach® (www.strategiccoach.com), an organization focused on helping entrepreneurs reach new levels of success and happiness. At the time, I was struggling to break through the "ceiling of complexity," a term Sullivan uses to describe what happens when entrepreneurs find themselves bogged down in activities that are boring, frustrating, and exhausting. The Strategic Coach® Program continues to play an important role in the way I think, act, and feel about my business and personal life, as well as how I interact with others.

A key principle in Sullivan's teachings is the concept of what he calls "Unique Ability®," a way of describing a powerful force that is at the very core of who you are as an individual. It is the essence of what you love to do and do best. Unique Ability® consists of your personal talents, passions, and skills. Sullivan asserts that every person has a Unique Ability®, but most people are not aware that they do. Because of this lack of awareness, these people have not experienced the infinite rewards that come from being able to harness and develop their natural talents and pursue their passions wholeheartedly. The more you are able to recognize your Unique Ability® and shape your life around it, the more freedom, success, and happiness you will experience.

According to Sullivan, each person's Unique Ability® has these four characteristics:

1. It's a superior ability that other people notice and value.

2. You love doing it and want to do it as much as possible.

3. It's energizing for you and others around you.

4. You keep getting better, never running out of possibilities for further improvement.

The synergistic effects of these four characteristics will give you enhanced confidence, inspiration, and motivation as you gain clarity about your Unique Ability®.

Most of us are not able to identify our Unique Ability®, let alone concentrate on it, however, because we are trapped by an erroneous notion we all learn at a young age: namely, that the secret to success in life is working on our weaknesses! Unfortunately, the focus on weaknesses results in failure, guilt, and loss of confidence. As a further result, our lives are filled with frustration, wasted potential, and missed opportunity. Moving beyond your lack of abilities to focus instead on the things you love is an important secret to maximizing your performance.

Through Dan Sullivan's teachings, I learned that people spend their lives in one of four zones of activity: incompetence, competence, excellence, and Unique Ability®. Here is my brief paraphrase of the four zones Sullivan has identified:

**Incompetent Activities:** Tasks that make you feel frustrated and stressed because you are just not good at them. What incompetent activities would you be happy to get rid of? What incompetent tasks drain your energy?

**Competent Activities:** Activities you are merely adequate at performing. A lot of people could do these tasks with greater success and less effort than you can. It is competent activities that create boredom in your life.

**Excellent Activities:** The activities you have superior skill in performing. People can count on you to accomplish these tasks. You may have even developed a reputation for your capability in these areas. However, deep down, you do not have a burning passion for these things. Even with all of the external positive reinforcement, these activities do not fuel your passion.

**Unique Ability® Activities:** Activities that enhance your confidence and create energy as well as enthusiasm are your Unique Ability® activities. When you engage in them, you bubble over with excitement. You could do these activities all day long and never grow bored. They give you endless possibilities for improvement, no matter how skilled you are at them.

Your success or failure in life depends on how much time you spend in each of these zones of activity. Unsuccessful people spend most of their time in the incompetent zone. High performers spend most of their time in the zones of competence and excellence. And peak performers—those who achieve extraordinary results during their lives—spend almost all of their time in the Unique Ability® zone. Sir James Matthew Barrie, the Scottish author, dramatist, and creator of Peter Pan, once said, "The secret to happiness is not doing what one likes, but liking what one does."

## DISCOVERING YOUR UNIQUE ABILITY®

How do you discover your Unique Ability®? How do you identify tasks that fill you with excitement, passion, and purpose? And, conversely, how do you systematically identify activities that consume your life and drain your energy?

I would like to suggest that you begin with the following five-step Unique Ability® Process:

1. **Unique Ability® Question:** Begin by asking yourself what activities give you energy, purpose, and passion. Consider asking other people who know you the same question.

2. **Unique Ability® Habits:** Begin by listing the things that you do automatically to produce your best results. These are the habits you have developed over the course of your lifetime. Pick the ones that reflect your core values.

3. **Unique Ability® Statement**: Consider expressing your Unique Ability® in one sentence. Begin with words such as "My Unique Ability® is characterized by my superior ability to . . ."

4. **Unique Ability® Future:** Envision yourself at some point in the future spending 100 percent of your time on your Unique Ability®. This skill is a powerful part of the process of becoming clear about your ideal future. Visioning is understood and appreciated by top athletes, entertainers, and successful people in all walks of life. Visioning your Unique Ability® will give you a sense of clarity, confidence, purpose, and passion.

5. **Unique Ability® Goal Setting:** Consider the positive implications of goal setting. Goal setting is a powerful part of the process of becoming clear about your ideal future, designing an action plan to get there, launching into action, and persisting until you reach your destination. This final step of the Unique Ability® process is crucial. (The concepts of visioning and goal setting will be covered in more detail in chapter 3.)

I would also like to recommend that you consider an assessment instrument called the Kolbe A Index™. Developed by Kathy Kolbe, this unique index is a proven and reliable tool to assess your instinctive and natural approach to creative problem solving. It is different from any other mental measurement tool because there are no right or wrong or good or bad answers.

Kolbe's definition of success is the freedom to be yourself, to appreciate your natural talents, and harness these talents to guide you to your peak. Your ability to understand what these talents are—especially your Unique Ability®—will allow you to be highly motivated, creative, and focused.

The Kolbe A Index™ determines a person's natural advantage according to the degree of intensity exhibited in each of the four action modes. In her book, *Conative Connection*, Kathy Kolbe tells us a fascinating story about the Phoenix Suns professional basketball team. Sitting in the Phoenix Coliseum one night, Kathy cringed as she saw her team lose yet another game. She could see that the talented players were being reined in, their instincts crushed by their coach. Knowing how to enhance human performance, Kathy called the Suns' general manager the next day to offer her services. Within two basketball seasons, with a new coach who understood the power of instinctive action, the Suns moved from near the cellar of the league to a force to be reckoned with. (See Figure 1.1.)

One hundred percent of your mental energy and creativity is distributed across the action modes listed in the figure. A corresponding number from 1 to 10 in the Kolbe A Index™ determines your mode of operation, or modus operandi (MO). As you discover your unique MO, you begin to understand and

| | |
|---|---|
| **Fact Finder** | The way you gather and share information. If you are a Fact Finder, you are precise, judicious, and thorough. You have a natural talent for dealing with detail and complexity. |
| **Follow Through** | The way you sort or store information. If your natural strength is Follow Through, you are focused and structured. You gain energy when bringing order and efficiency to a project, and you are meticulous at planning, programing, and designing. |
| **Quick Start** | The way you deal with risk and uncertainty. If you are a Quick Start, you have an affinity for risk. You tend to be especially spontaneous and intuitive, flexible and fluent with ideas. You thrive in an atmosphere of challenge and change. |
| **Implementer** | The way you handle space and tangible solutions. If your natural strength is one of being an Implementer, you enjoy being hands-on and craft-oriented. You have a strong sense of three-dimensional form and substance and the ability to lead with the concrete. |

Figure 1.1: The Four Action Modes

appreciate your instinctive, or natural, ways of taking action. Figure 1.2 is a representation of my Kolbe A Index™ of 5762.

As you can see, I possess a natural talent for "follow through" yet also have positive instincts for fact finding and being a quick start. The Kolbe A Index™ has allowed me to understand that I have a natural advantage when arranging, designing, scheduling, and planning. It is an important first step in allowing you to discover your Unique Ability®. As Kathy Kolbe writes of Abraham Maslow, the guru of self-actualization, he discovered that a person seeks "to be true to his or her own nature, to trust him or herself, to be authentic, spontaneous, honestly expressive, and to look for sources in his or her actions."

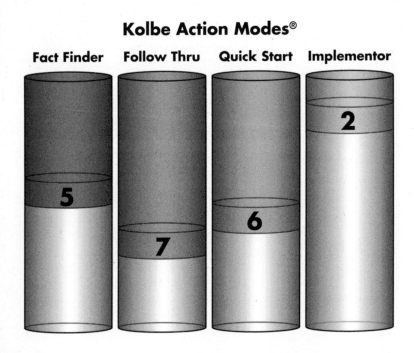

## Kolbe Action Modes®

Figure 1.2: The author's Kolbe Action Modes Assessment

As a perfectionist, I often have a difficult time letting go of projects that do not reflect my Unique Ability®. For example, while I am a capable account manager, my Unique Ability® is articulating the value proposition of The Addis Group and Addis Intellectual Capital. Far too often, I get mired in day-to-day account management responsibilities when I should be conveying each of the firms' unique messages in the marketplace. When this occurs, I frustrate myself as well as those people who support me.

## Focus on Your Natural Advantage and Uniqueness; Delegate Everything Else

Peak performers focus on their natural advantage and Unique Ability® and delegate everything else. These individuals hand off work to others who possess a Unique Ability® in the areas to be delegated. There are people sitting around you today who each possess a mental energy and creativity that differs from yours. Tasks that drain your energy will fill the bucket for them.

///////////

If you're frustrated, bored, and losing energy, it's imperative that you discover your natural strengths and Unique Ability®. Furthermore, assessing these attributes is critical to the process of planning where you want to go in your life and how you're going to get there. Discovering your natural strengths and Unique Ability® is essential for the climb you have ahead of you so you can reach the summit!

# CHAPTER 2

# Finding Your Passion

*There comes that mysterious meeting in life when
someone acknowledges who we are and what we can be,
igniting the circuits of our highest potential.*
**—Rusty Berkus**

Just as important as knowing your natural strengths and your Unique Ability® is discovering your passions and interests—knowing where your emotional energy resides—before you set out on your climb.

Business consultants spend a lot of time trying to understand sales performance. This includes, but is not limited to, an analysis of prospecting, sales skills, and customer relationship management. The consultant's performance indicators focus on a host of quantifiable and activity-based measures, including the number of prospect calls, point-of-sale proposals, cross-selling initiatives, and retention.

True, performance can be enhanced through these strategies, activities, and measures. And there is no question that a strategic business development plan that incorporates a differentiated sales process is essential. But what is often overlooked in the analytical process is emotional energy—your passion for the business.

In *The 21 Indispensable Qualities of a Leader*, John Maxwell states, "If you look at the lives of effective leaders, you will find that they often don't fit into a stereotypical mold. For example, more than 50 percent of all CEOs of Fortune 500 companies had a C or C- average in college. Nearly 75 percent of all U.S. presidents were in the bottom half of their school classes. And more than 50 percent of all millionaire entrepreneurs never finished college."

Similar observations can be seen in *Time* magazine's 2013 list of the "100 Most Influential People in the World." While each person no doubt had been blessed with talent, it was apparent that their desire, supported by purpose and passion, served as the fuel for their ultimate success. When you think about influential leaders, you will be struck by their passion: Gandhi for human rights, Winston Churchill for freedom, Martin Luther King Jr. for equality, Bill Gates for technology. Influential leaders have a burning desire to make a difference.

Thus, in order for apparently "ordinary" people to achieve great things, they need passion.

Very broadly, passion is defined as "a strong or intense feeling or emotion." It is the fuel for your will. Passion creates powerful energy. Typically, passion begins as a focused desire but eventually swallows all of the emotions it engenders. For example, if you want something badly enough, you will find the willpower to achieve it.

Historically, expressing passion in the traditional business setting was considered unprofessional. There was a belief that the display of emotion in a business deal could jeopardize the outcome or at least make the transaction less productive. Times have changed, however. In fact, many of today's notable business leaders are emotional people—Jack Welch, Michael Dell, and Mark Cuban, to name but a few.

Passion in business translates into loving what you do. No business professional should feel guilty for sharing his or her emotions. After all, humans are emotional creatures. The key lies in learning how to *harness* and *direct* your passion so that it serves you in positive ways. When you follow your passion, you will become a more dedicated and productive person, and your passion will positively impact others around you. Your passion will have a measurable and sustainable impact on those whom you touch. While it is important that you demonstrate enthusiasm for your corporate culture, it is just as important that you show passion for your products, services, and resources. Consumers take genuine interest in people who demonstrate excitement and enthusiasm about what they deliver.

Likewise, consumers make buying decisions based, in large part, on passion. In fact, leading marketers use words and images to evoke emotions so as to create enduring psychological bonds between the customer and a product or service. Brand consultants often refer to the passionately strong brands of such companies as Urban Outfitters, Harley-Davidson, Starbucks, Krispy Kreme, and eBay.

In the business world, passion comes from an influential leader's belief in his or her company's value proposition and unique way through which the company creates value for those whom it serves.

Referring once again to Maxwell's insights about essential leadership qualities, he highlights these four truths about passion:

1. Passion is a first step to achievement;

2. Passion increases willpower;

3. Passion changes you;

4. Passion makes the impossible possible.

Over the years, numerous colleagues and clients have commented on the emotion I put into each and every business endeavor. I can personally attest to Maxwell's four truths. My passion has had a profound impact on my performance.

## YOUR PASSION INDEX

Your purpose is what fuels your passion. And your passion is the fuel for the fire in your heart and soul. It impacts your life and those around you. "A leader with great passion and few skills always outperforms a leader with great skills and no passion," says Maxwell. You cannot reach the peak without a clear appreciation for and understanding of your Passion Index.

What is your Passion Index? Think of it as the thermostat that measures the intensity of your emotions. To help you determine your Passion Index, take a minute to agree or disagree with the following three statements:

1. I cannot sleep because I get so excited about a new business system, strategy, or tool.

2. I find myself getting excited when I share my unique business model.

3. My energy is contagious.

////////////

If you agreed with all three of these assertions, you have a high Passion Index. Congratulations! If you did not, do not despair. While there is no magic pill for passion, it will be drawn out of you as you dare to be different in developing a vision and setting your goals, as you create your unique value proposition, and as you build your relationship network. Let's look at your vision for the future and your short- and long-term goals in the next couple of chapters.

# CHAPTER 3

# Identifying Your Vision, Setting Your Goals

*You control your future, your destiny. What you think about comes about. By recording your dreams and goals on paper, you set in motion the process of becoming the person you most want to be. Put your future in good hands—your own.*

**—Mark Victor Hansen**

Your ability to create a vision and set goals is essential to your personal and professional lives. A vision allows you to see yourself at some point in the future, while goals offer a road map to reach that point. There is nothing more rewarding than having a vision, setting goals to reach that vision, and making the vision become reality. Visioning and goal setting are foundational competencies you will draw on as you plan, prepare, and pack for your journey to reach the peak.

## MIRACLE IN THE MAKING:
## THE STORY OF ADAM TALIAFERRO

Perhaps there is no better story about visioning and goal setting than that of Adam Taliaferro. In 2000, he joined the Penn State football team as one of the top-rated players in the country. He had been a standout running back and cornerback for the Eastern High School Vikings in Voorhees Township, New Jersey. In just two years of varsity football, he averaged 9.4 yards per carry, racking up sixty-two touchdowns and seven interceptions. He had also been a four-year starter in basketball and set his school's record in the high jump at 6 feet 6 inches. At Penn State, he earned playing time for Joe Paterno's Nittany Lions despite the coach's well-documented tendency to redshirt freshman players.

On September 23, 2000, while he was playing in only the fifth game of his college career, Taliaferro's spine was crushed while he was tackling Ohio State's tailback Jerry Westbrooks. Taliaferro's helmet hit Westbrooks's knee during the tackle, bursting the fifth cervical vertebra in his neck and bruising his spinal cord. Taliaferro was unable to control his fall, and when the crown of his helmet hit the turf, his body rolled awkwardly over his neck. Taliaferro was paralyzed on the hit, which left him with no movement from the neck down.

Fortunately, he received immediate medical attention and later underwent spinal fusion surgery at the Ohio State University Medical Center. Although the surgery was successful, he was given only a 3 percent chance of ever walking again. On October 6, 2000, he began his well-publicized rehab at Magee Rehabilitation Hospital in Philadelphia.

ESPN's Rick Reilly recalled the Adam Taliaferro story in a January 23, 2012, article titled "Joe Paterno's True Legacy."

He lay on the September field paralyzed and panicked. The first person he saw when he opened his eyes was Paterno. "He could see I was losing it, but his eyes stayed totally calm," Taliaferro recalls. "And I remember that familiar, high-pitched voice going, 'You're going to get through this, Kid. You're going to be okay.' And I just trusted him. I believed it."

While Taliaferro was lying in a hospital bed in Philadelphia, everything frozen solid below his neck, Paterno would fly to Philly every other week to see him. "He'd bring in our trainer and a couple of teammates," Taliaferro said. "Nobody in the hospital knew he was there. I can't tell you what that meant to me. I'm stuck in that hospital and here's Coach Paterno bringing a piece of the team to me, in the midst of the season. How many coaches would do that?"

One midnight, Taliaferro moved a toe and the first person his dad called was Paterno. Andre Taliaferro held the phone to Adam's ear and Paterno said, "You're going to prove 'em all wrong, Kid!" From then on, every visit, Paterno wanted to see Taliaferro move something new. "I got to where I wanted to be ready. A finger, a hand, whatever. I wanted to perform for Coach Paterno."

One day, five months into it, Paterno walked in and said, "What's new, Kid?" Taliaferro swung his legs over the bed, stood and extended his hand to shake. "I'll never forget his eyes. They were already huge behind those Coke-bottled glasses, but they got even bigger," stated Taliaferro. Paterno gave him a 10-second hug and said, "Kid, ya make me proud."

After eight months of rehab, Taliaferro learned to walk again. He returned to Penn State less than a year after his injury, leading the Nittany Lions onto Beaver Stadium's Field for the first game of the 2001 season against the Miami Hurricanes in front of a record crowd of 109,313.

It was actually during high school that Taliaferro had learned about the power of visioning and goal setting. Before every athletic event, he would visualize a successful performance. He also was goal oriented. Little did he know then that these skills would change the outcome of his life just a few years later. Today, Adam Taliaferro's poem "When I Walk" is displayed in the Penn State Sports Museum. With his generous permission, I have reprinted it here in this discussion about having a vision that keeps us moving forward—sometimes against impossible odds.

*When I Walk*

*When I walk, it's for those who prayed for me.*
*When I walk, it's for the tremendous amount of love and support my parents showed me.*
*When I walk, it's for the therapists at Magee who pushed me through each day of rehab.*
*When I walk, it's for the doctors who saved me.*
*When I walk, it's for the alumnus who made me truly feel like a part of the Penn State Family.*

*When I walk, it's for my friends who visited me each week in the hospital.*

*When I walk, it's for my little brother who became my big brother in my time of need.*

*When I walk, it's for those I never met, but gave something just to let me know they cared.*

*When I walk, it's for everyone in my entire family.*

*When I walk, it's for my teammates here at Penn State who stuck by me the whole way.*

*When I walk, it's for PENN STATE.*

Sam Carchidi chronicles Taliaferro's life and recovery in *Miracle in the Making*, published in 2001. After graduating from Penn State, Taliaferro earned a law degree and practiced with the law firm of Duane Morris. In September 2012, he joined the pharmaceutical company Bristol-Myers Squibb as a healthcare advocate.

Taliaferro is passionate about servant leadership and community support, as evidenced by his nonprofit organization, The Adam Taliaferro Foundation (www.taliaferrofoundation.org), which helps student athletes with spinal injuries. He is a gifted motivational speaker who continues to touch all who come in contact with him. In recognition of his commitment to serving others, Taliaferro was the recipient of the Philadelphia Sports Writers Association Humanitarian Award. In the spring of 2012, he was elected to the board of trustees at his alma mater.

On a personal note, I am proud to call Adam a friend. He continues to inspire my family, my staff, and me in our journey to the peak. Adam is a living testament to the value of visioning and goal setting.

## THE ART OF GOAL SETTING

Goal setting is a powerful process to turn your vision into reality. It encompasses becoming clear about your ideal future, designing an action plan to get you there, launching into action, and persisting until you reach your destination. The better you understand what you are capable of, the more on-target, realistic, and achievable your goals will be.

Top athletes, entertainers, and successful people in all walks of life understand and appreciate the art of goal setting. A person who learns how to set goals lives each day with a sense of clarity, confidence, purpose, and passion.

I was first introduced to the art of goal setting in the early 1980s while maturing as an account manager at Johnson & Higgins in Philadelphia. Rather than seeing it as a chore, I learned that the process of goal setting was stimulating, energizing, and rewarding. I vividly recall asking myself questions such as these: Which goal will give me the most energy? Which goal am I most committed to? What goal offers the most value to me? And, in three years, how important will this or that goal be? Goal setting made a lot of sense to me. Without goals, I would have no sense of direction.

The art of goal setting will enable you to

- Decide what is important in your life;
- Determine what you want to achieve;
- Separate what is important from what is irrelevant;
- Be motivated;
- Facilitate your ability to benchmark progress;

- Gain self-confidence when your goals become your reality.

Think of goal setting as your navigation system. Goal setting allows you to identify what is important in your life and turn your thoughts and ideas into specific, actionable, and measurable actions. Importantly, your goals will protect you from becoming distracted by other people's agendas and expectations. In designing your goal-setting navigation system and charting your own course, you will have control over the process of reaching your destination—the summit.

Most successful people are goal oriented. They have learned how to turn their vision into action. They have a knack for bringing the future into the present so they can take action now. Greg Norman, the legendary golfer, put it this way: "Setting goals for your game is an art. The trick is setting them at the right level, neither too low nor too high. A good goal should be lofty enough to inspire hard work yet realistic enough to provide solid hope of attainment." Because your journey will require you to master the art of goal setting, you will want to recall Norman's quote as you ascend the path to reach your peak.

A common acronym used in the process of setting goals is SMART. The S stands for specific. M is for measurable. A stands for achievable. R is for realistic. T stands for time bound. Think of a goal as a dream with a timeline. Every goal needs a target date for completion.

As you design specific, measurable, achievable, realistic goals to be attained within a certain timeline, take care not to lose sight of your big-picture goals—your future vision. SMART goals can help you climb the ladder of success step-by-step, but without the end in view you could find that you have leaned your ladder against the wrong wall.

If you approach goal setting with a random mind-set, the impact will be minimal. It is essential that your goal-setting process be strategic. A few years back, I created a visioning and goal-setting system entitled Performance Map 365™. Although it was originally designed as a system to enhance my performance, the tool is now being utilized by hundreds of individuals whom I serve as coach and mentor. Performance Map 365™ enhances one's ability to create visions, set goals, benchmark progress, analyze personal and business goals, build a relational network, better understand one's Unique Ability®, establish objectives as related to delegation, and work through frustrations. The following five-step strategy is contained within Performance Map 365™.

## Step 1: List your goals A to Z.

The art of goal setting begins with writing your personal and professional goals from A to Z. Don't hold back and don't edit yourself. Write down whatever comes to your mind. Go nuts and take pride in the length and diversity of your list. This exercise gives you energy and motivation. It's also fun.

Some of your goals will be short-term while others will focus on the future. Don't worry about that. Just list goals that are important to you. You may wish to ask yourself the following questions:

- What is my purpose and mission in life?

- How do I want to focus my time and energy?

- What are my developmental needs at this point in my life?

- What does my ideal lifestyle look like?

I've found that answering these four questions adds clarity, simplicity, purpose, and passion to the goal-setting process.

Your goals will cover a wide range of categories: among them are family, career, education, finances, physical health, spiritual nurture, community service, etc. The A to Z exercise will allow you to create a whole picture of what is important to you and what you want to do with your life. Many of your A to Z goals will be lifetime goals.

## Step 2: Prioritize your goals.

After you have gone through the A to Z exercise, begin rating your goals on a scale of 1 to 10, with 10 being most significant to you at this point in time, and 1 meaning it is not a priority right now. Here are a few questions that should help you prioritize your goals:

- Which goal(s) will give me the most energy?

- Which goal(s) am I most committed to?

- What goal (or goals) offers the most value to me?

- What goal (or goals) is fully within my control?

- How important will this goal be to me five years from now?

The process of prioritizing your goals will allow you to break down your A to Z list into smaller targets. You will gain great clarity through this exercise.

## Step 3: Set your execution strategy and achievement time frame.

By prioritizing your goals, you have set the stage for an execution strategy through which you are able to define the following plans: lifetime plan, five-year plan, one-year plan, ninety-day plan, and weekly plan. Your lifetime and five-year plans represent your vision of the future—that is, the essential points of your long-term destination. These big-picture plans are vital. However, it will be your ability to execute the weekly, ninety-day, and one-year goals that will launch you toward your ideal future.

Your one-year goals should be the kind that requires you to stretch your capabilities, increase your resources, and make meaningful improvements to your personal and business lives. Your one-year plan should be power packed, including relevant, motivational, and realistic steps on the path to attaining your long-term vision. The ninety-day plan supports the one-year goals, an essential means to benchmark your progress, reevaluate your priorities, and make sure that you are focused on what matters most. It's not easy to reach your one-year goals without setting and reaching ninety-day plans.

As I look back at my career, the weekly plan has likewise been an essential key to my success. I have made it a habit to come to work each week with a plan to accomplish specific objectives that support my ninety-day and one-year plans, as well as my big-picture future vision.

## Step 4: Practice the art of visualization.

Mental imagery, or visualization, is a key component of successful goal setting. By visualization I mean your ability to see yourself at the point of achieving your goal. Goal setting breaks down unless you have great clarity about your vision. Visualization is a mental technique that uses imagination to make dreams and goals come true. It is a power that can alter your environment and circumstances, causing events to happen. How does it work, and why? The subconscious mind accepts the thoughts that you often repeat. When it accepts them, it changes your mind-set accordingly, as well as your habits and actions.

I use visualization each and every day. I find it especially helpful for speeches and key client presentations, as well as for my athletic endeavors.

## Step 5: Celebrate achieving your goals.

When you achieve a goal, take time to enjoy the satisfaction of what you have accomplished. The execution of a strategy deserves special attention. Congratulate yourself on staying the course and for all the time and effort you put into each step. Celebrate the moment and absorb the implication of the goal as it relates to your journey to the summit. If your goal is a significant one, reward yourself appropriately.

///////////

On occasion, you will not accomplish a given goal. You must not lose confidence or get frustrated. The failure to actualize a specific goal is not important as long as you gave it your best effort and learned a lesson from the process. Revered CBS news anchor Walter Cronkite once said, "I can't imagine a person becoming a success who doesn't give this game of life everything he's got."

The art of goal setting is one of your most important life skills. The process will ignite your passion for the future. And it will help give your ascent to the summit much-needed structure and direction.

# CHAPTER 4

# Balancing Your Work with Your Life

*It is one of the most beautiful compensations of this life that no man can sincerely try to help another without helping himself.*
**—Ralph Waldo Emerson**

Do you have a proper balance between your personal and business lives? Or are the demands of your work infringing upon the quantity and quality of time you have with family, friends, hobbies, and community? Before you depart for the summit, assess this key issue and consider how to keep your life in balance while working so hard to reach the peak of your potential.

The following quiz will tell you the degree to which you should be concerned about your current work-life balance:

1. I work sixty or more hours per week.
2. I have little personal downtime.

**3.** I am exhausted when I get home from work.

**4.** I seem to have precious little time to enhance my personal relationships.

**5.** I think the word "fun" is no longer in my vocabulary.

I am embarrassed to admit that I answered yes to all five statements the first time I took the quiz. Work-life balance remains my biggest challenge in my quest to reach the peak. If you answered yes to two or more of the statements above, you owe it to yourself to learn more about this issue as well.

The term "work-life balance" first appeared in the 1970s. The expression means having equilibrium among all the priorities in your life. It's interesting to note that this state of balance differs from person to person. However, if there is little or no balance over an extended period of time, the vast majority of people get caught in the stages of the stress cycle (see Figure 4.1.) and, eventually, burn out.

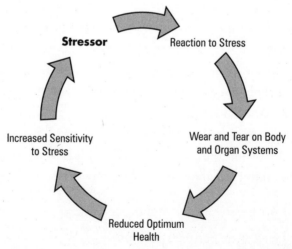

Figure 4.1: Stress Cycle

As this graphic illustrates, stress begins with a stressor—the cause of the stress. Our stressors in life include, but are not limited to, work deadlines, personality conflicts, and sick relatives. Unfortunately, in life you will always have stressors.

Our reaction to stress begins with how we perceive it emotionally. What is a major calamity to one person is no big deal to another.

Research substantiates that stress puts wear and tear on our bodies and organ systems in many ways. The same stress reactions that at first help you to cope soon begin to wear you down. Everything from tight neck muscles, headaches, exhaustion, increased colds, and insomnia are impacted by stress.

After a sustained period of chronic stress with little or no relief, we experience reduced optimum health. This is shown in serious diseases like high blood pressure, heart problems, diabetes, skin conditions, asthma, arthritis, depression, and even cancer.

While your body is wearing down and fighting disease and your emotions are worn and exhausted, your sensitivity to stress increases. This is why people often "fly off the handle" at very small events.

And the cycle continues. A smaller and smaller stressor will initiate the same stress reaction that a big event used to get.

Research indicates that the workplace has become the single greatest source of stress for men and women. Let's look at a handful of scenarios that create stress in the workplace. Do any of these statements apply to you?

- I have little impact on or control over the decision making in my department.

- My expectations of my own work performance do not meet my superiors' expectations.

- I have little opportunity for growth, development, or promotion at my company.

- My workload is very heavy, requiring long hours and infrequent breaks.

- My role is not clearly defined.

- I do not feel that the level of communication within my firm meets my needs.

- I am involved in routine tasks that offer little or no professional stimulation.

- My work environment is unpleasant.

Today's intense, competitive business climate has created corporate cultures that demand more and more from their people. If an ambitious person wants to get ahead, he or she is looking at sixty- to seventy-hour workweeks as the new standard. Work overload has been exacerbated by computer technologies that were intended to make our lives easier. Technology advances now require that people view most professions as 24/7 businesses, which makes the achievement of work-life balance very challenging.

Your own journey to the summit will be very demanding. At times you will be pushed to the limits, so it is essential that you learn strategies to help you achieve work-life balance.

## STRATEGIES TO HELP YOU ACHIEVE WORK-LIFE BALANCE

As you push the limits to reach your peak, it is important that you make room in your life to take care of your physical, mental, and emotional well-being. The following list features ten different strategies you should be aware of and try to implement as you attempt to balance all of the priorities of your life:

1. **Self-Awareness.** The first and most important step to take in achieving proper work-life balance is to understand the importance of harmonizing mind, body, and spirit. Being "self-aware" will allow you to monitor your stress levels, see danger signs, and take personal responsibility for your holistic health. As your self-awareness grows, you will gain a sense of confidence in managing your work-life balance.

2. **Support from Family and Friends**. In your quest for balance between your work life and your home life, there is perhaps no more important factor than your relationships with family and friends. Getting the family aspect of your life right will help you enormously in achieving and maintaining balance. Support and encouragement from friends is also essential. A good friend will listen, support, sympathize, and offer direction. He or she will be an important ally in your work-life balance struggle.

3. **Nutrition and Exercise.** Physical stamina is not a luxury in today's fast-paced business climate; it is a required element for high performance. Your mind and body cannot operate at full potential if you have poor nutritional habits. Exercise is equally essential to maintaining good health. Exercise is also an important strategy to help you work off stress. Choose an activity you enjoy. Possibly, one of your hobbies can be combined with an exercise program.

4. **Hobbies.** You may be so busy with work that you no longer have time for hobbies, but having even one hobby is essential to work-life balance. It lets you escape from the rigors of work to focus upon something you enjoy. Time completely absorbed in an activity unrelated to your business will do wonders for your productivity. It will also give your mind and body a well-deserved rest from work.

5. **Recovery Strategies.** Professional athletes and entertainers plan recovery cycles into their intense training programs. They understand that their mind and body need time to recuperate from strenuous activity. Work is no different. Your work-life balance plan should incorporate recovery breaks into your daily or weekly routine. These can be anything from a five-minute walk at lunchtime to dinner and a movie with family and friends to a weekend golf game.

6. **Sleep.** Sleep deprivation is a major issue for people under stress. If you make it a habit to skimp on sleep,

you may not even remember how it feels to wake up fully rested. Sleep is an essential ingredient in balancing work and home obligations. Make sleep a priority for a week and see how it impacts your performance.

7. **Stuff.** For many people, it is the "stuff" in their lives that causes stress. Stuff runs the spectrum from unfinished projects to personality clashes with coworkers to a messy office. Too much stuff depletes energy and causes stress and anxiety. Stop and recognize all the stuff in your life. You will gain immediate confidence and clarity as you begin to identify and remove unneeded stuff from your life.

8. **Learn How to Say No.** High achievers get ahead by taking on projects and handling them efficiently and effectively. Far too often, the same high achievers are the go-to people in the office. It is logical. If a high achiever is so good at projects, let him or her handle more and more problems and issues. If you are a high achiever, you must learn how to say no. Do not let someone else's problem or responsibility become yours.

9. **Time Management.** You have heard the term "time management" a thousand times. You may not have a time management issue; rather, you have become so conditioned to multitasking that you have forgotten to do just one thing at a time. Interestingly, current studies have revealed that multitasking is really a myth: the human mind can really do only one thing

at a time, and what we think is multitasking is just rapid switching between activities, which makes our performance on all of them less effective. Your ability to focus on one issue at a time will reduce anxiety and stress.

10. **Rearranging Priorities.** Work-life balance means having equilibrium among all of the priorities of your life. Consider this simple exercise. List the priorities of your life from 1 to 5. Your priorities may include personal interests, family time, hobbies, exercise, or numerous other things. Now, analyze the percentage of time you actually spend on these priorities. It is likely that you will experience frustration from the fact that your ranking of these priorities is out of alignment with the actual time you spend on them. Reviewing your priorities, allotting time to each activity in proportion to its importance, and designing a plan to measure progress are all important components of your work-life balance plan.

Balancing your professional and personal lives is essential for a rewarding career. It will make the journey to your summit much more enjoyable and memorable, too. You owe it to yourself to make sure that the proper balance is in place.

Let me share a personal experience to illustrate the importance of work-life balance. My wife, Bobbie, and I are the proud parents of three boys. Andrew and Jeff were born in 1981 and 1983. They were seven and nine years old when I ventured out on my own to start The Addis Group, an insurance brokerage and risk management consulting firm in Philadelphia. Will, the youngest, was born just twenty-seven days after the firm opened its doors in 1990.

As you likely know, the demands of a start-up business are immense. The Addis Group required long hours, amazing focus, and a 24/7 mentality. Although I did not realize it at the time, this 24/7 mentality would impact the quantity and quality of time I spent with my boys. While Bobbie worked weekends as a registered nurse in Philadelphia-based hospitals, Andrew, Jeff, and Will had a standard routine of joining Dad in the office. In an attempt to stay occupied, the boys invented games like miniature golf between office cubicles and copy machine adventures. I was with them in body and spirit—yet so distant. I now realize that I began my journey to the peak with little or no workplace–home life balance.

While Bobbie and the three boys were impacted in different ways, I vividly recall a situation with Jeffrey, my middle son, that occurred when he was eleven years old. The firm's largest client, a hospitality management company with dozens of full-service hotels throughout the United States, asked me to carry a beeper at all times to respond to the safety and risk management concerns of its general managers.

Upon returning home late one evening from a demanding day at work, I placed my wallet, keys, and the beeper on the counter in the kitchen. After eating dinner, I noticed that the beeper was missing. When I asked my family if they had seen it, I saw something in Jeffrey's face. When I confronted him, he admitted throwing the beeper into the woods behind our home. His comment was: "I don't want to live with a beeper. I want to live with my dad." In the dark of the night, the beeper was found and our relationship mended. However, the beeper story still serves as a reminder of the critical importance of work-life balance.

////////////

Your journey to the peak will be extremely demanding. It will require tremendous focus time and effort. As you progress to the summit, it will be essential that you have balance in all the priorities of your life.

# Setting Up Base Camp (Preparing to Present Yourself to Others)

*There have been joys too great to be described in words, and there have been griefs upon which I have not dared to dwell, and with these in mind I say, climb if you will, but remember that courage and strength are naught without prudence, and that a momentary negligence may destroy the happiness of a lifetime. Do nothing in haste, look well to each step, and from the beginning think what may be the end.*

**—Edward Whymper**

In climbing, the base camp is a location partway up the mountain where the climbing party sets up a headquarters from which to mount their full assault of the summit. It's where food, equipment, and other supplies essential to the safe and successful completion of the mission are stored. It's also where the climbers establish a communication center, first aid facility, and other support services fundamental to the trip.

In undertaking the adventure to reach your peak—your full potential—it's imperative that you set up your own version of a base camp before taking on the challenge of the assault, whether your personal challenge is in the form of further career development, attaining status in your organization, or launching a business and finding clients. Your camp needs to consist of foundational provisions that will anchor, support, and sustain you throughout your journey. In your career and life, essential provisions include self-confidence, service to others, a unique message, relationships, the right mentor, and emotional intelligence.

The following six chapters will discuss these base camp essentials to help you gain a solid footing and an advantageous position from which to press on to your summit.

# CHAPTER 5

# Gaining Confidence

*Your chances of success in any undertaking can always
be measured by your belief in yourself.*
**—Robert Collier**

As a business advisor and a coach, I have the unique opportunity to interact with people from all walks of life. People in different stages of development. People of diverse industries. People with different roles and responsibilities. I have discovered a commonality with all of these people: their performance rarely reflects their potential. And this gap causes frustration, disappointment, and most notably, loss of confidence.

Furthermore, this lack of confidence prevents people from taking steps to close the gap. Self-confidence is an attitude characterized by the positive belief that you can take control of your life and of your plans. It's a belief in your own abilities. People who are self-confident are those who acknowledge their capacity to do something and then proceed to do those things—no matter what other people may say. They don't need the approval of others to affirm their worth as an individual. People who are self-confident take advantage of opportunities that come their way.

Self-confidence can be a self-fulfilling prophecy, as those without it may fail or not try because they lack it, and those with it may succeed because they have it.

You cannot reach your peak without confidence. To be successful, you must be confident in your approach, your communication skills, your team, your technical know-how, and the manner in which you deliver your services and resources. Plus, you must remain confident in the face of rejection. Learning how to be confident is the single most important life skill you will ever acquire. It impacts your happiness, success, and well-being. Confidence is the foundation for *all* other desirable qualities.

Historically, confidence was thought of as an innate personal trait: some were born with it, whereas others were not. However, more recent research substantiates that confidence is learned and developed. Nobody is born with confidence. You develop confidence while growing up. The role of parents in installing self-confidence in their children is essential. Parents who are critical of their children without acknowledging their strengths unknowingly damage the development of self-confidence. On the other hand, parents who give support and encouragement are far more likely to rear self-confident children.

Henry Ford captured the essence of self-confidence when he said, "If you think you can, you can. If you think you can't, you are right." Knowing how to be self-confident is all about believing in yourself. To grow to be confident starts with the willingness to accept small challenges, which gradually builds to accepting bigger ones. Confidence is built one step at a time. You must realize that even those people who appear to be self-confident acquire this trait over time. You acquire confidence through the development of three attributes that interact with one another:

1. **Knowledge:** education, research, analysis, investigation, observation, and, most important, firsthand experience;

2. **Skill:** the ability to effectively utilize knowledge;

3. **Attitude:** your belief that you have the ability to control outcomes.

In learning how to be confident, it is essential for you to understand that confidence is under your control. It is not controlled by someone else.

Self-confidence is about balance. There are people with low self-confidence. At the other extreme, there are people who are overly confident. Overconfident people often take too much risk, stretching themselves beyond their capabilities and eventually running into roadblocks. Overconfidence is having unmerited confidence, believing that one is capable when this is not the case. The term "choking" refers to losing confidence, especially self-confidence, just at the moment when it is needed the most—and doing poorly as a result.

Confident people risk security and comfort to achieve higher levels of growth and independence. They have the ability to see obstacles as opportunities. Each day begins and ends with a sense of clarity, simplicity, and purpose. Figure 5.1 lists the traits that correspond to being an individual with high self-confidence and one with low self-confidence.

| High Self-confidence | Low Self-confidence |
|---|---|
| Belief that outcomes can be controlled and impacted. | Belief that individual actions have little or no impact on outcomes. |
| Willing to take risks and go outside the boundaries of one's comfort zone. | Stays within one's comfort zone. Avoids risks wherever possible. |
| Admits mistakes and learns from them. | Fears failure. Covers up mistakes. Fixes problems before anyone becomes aware. |
| Does what he or she believes is right, even under criticism. | Behaves in a manner conducive to what the majority think. |
| Does not need continual positive reinforcement. | Needs praise and positive reinforcement. |

Figure 5.1: Self-confidence traits

Sadly, people with low self-confidence live in a vicious cycle. Their lack of confidence makes it difficult for them to achieve success, and their inability to experience success brings on negativity. People with low self-confidence live in the daily condition of anxiety, confusion, and fatigue. Their self-image is one of paralysis and an inability to live with a sense of purpose and passion.

Highly self-confident people feel in control. They have the

ability to shut out distractions, establish priorities, make sound judgments, and create strategies to carry them out effectively. They make good use of their strengths and resources. Most important, self-confident individuals possess an ability to create value for themselves and those around them.

In an increasingly complex and turbulent world, it's easy to lose confidence in your ability to control the outcomes of your actions. The psychologist Martin Seligman originated the term "learned helplessness" to describe the mental state of a person who perceives an absence of control over the outcome of a situation. This perceived lack of control leads to indecision and/or impulsive actions.

To the surprise of many who know me, I admit that I struggle with self-confidence. Although my track record would seem to indicate that I am a risk taker and willing to go outside my comfort zone, the reality is something quite different. I have a fear of failure, need praise and positive reinforcement, and work hard to feel in control. In the early stages of the evolution in building both The Addis Group and Addis Intellectual Capital, especially, I lacked confidence because I had never ventured down those paths before. As I began to take risks and move outside the boundaries of my comfort zone, however, I experienced the exhilaration of increased knowledge, skill, and attitude. I also surrounded myself with highly self-confident people who possess positive attitudes and who believe in me.

I can personally attest that gaining confidence is like riding a bicycle. At first you are tentative because you fear falling off. But you soon gain confidence with patience and practice. I suggest that you consider the following three-step approach—drawing on what you've read in the Elevation I chapters—to increasing your level of self-confidence:

1. Assess your natural strengths and Unique Ability®.

2. Visualize the tangible benefits that will result from the actions you take (fully aware that those actions may feel outside the boundaries of your comfort zone).

3. Reach for support and encouragement from those you trust as you consider "taking a risk."

///////////

You need self-confidence to reach the peak of your potential. In fact, being confident is the first step in climbing to the summit. Start by acknowledging your talents, avoiding situations that discourage you from gaining confidence, and seeking opportunities to enhance your self-confidence. Success breeds confidence. Confidence brings success.

# CHAPTER 6

# Cultivating Servant Leadership

*If your actions inspire others to dream more, learn more,*
*do more and become more, you are a leader.*

**—John Quincy Adams**

lmost no one scales a peak alone; it's nearly always a team effort. So, if there is one quality particularly essential to establishing a good base camp, it is servant leadership. I strongly believe this is the most important trait you should cultivate in order to reach your full potential.

Are you a servant leader? Is your top priority to look after the needs of your followers so as to ensure that they reach their full potential, hence perform at their best?

Robert K. Greenleaf (1904–1990) first coined the term "servant leadership" in his 1970 essay "The Servant as Leader." Since that time, more than half a million copies of his books and essays have been sold worldwide. Greenleaf's servant leadership writings have made a deep, long-lasting impression on many individuals and corporations that share a concern for the issues of leadership, management, service, and personal growth. His influence is also evidenced through the work of numerous award-winning authors, among them Stephen Covey, Ken Blanchard, and John Maxwell, to name a few.

## WHAT IS SERVANT LEADERSHIP?

Put simply, servant leaders serve the people they lead. Their style represents a selfless approach to leadership, one that places serving others—including business associates, customers, community, and country—as priority number one. Servant leadership promotes a sense of community and the sharing of power and decision making. Servant leaders understand that personal recognition is not the path toward team success. Their ego and individual goals do not get in the way of the larger picture of team goals.

The words "servant" and "leader" are usually thought of as opposites. However, when these two opposites are brought together, the powerful concept of the selfless leader emerges. At its core, servant leadership represents a transformational approach to life and work—a way of being that creates positive change in life, business, and society.

## WHAT DO SERVANT LEADERS DO DIFFERENTLY?

A servant leader serves first. He or she is the one who is the first to volunteer to help. A servant leader is never too proud to do the work—even the difficult or unpopular jobs—in order for the team to succeed. Often, the servant leader tackles those jobs without anyone knowing because there is no complaining involved.

Greenleaf put it this way in his now legendary essay: "Servant leadership begins with the natural feeling that one wants to serve. Then conscious choice brings one to aspire to lead. The best test is to ask oneself two questions: (1) Do those served grow as persons? (2) Do they, while being served, become healthier, wiser, freer, autonomous, more likely themselves to be servants?" Building upon Greenleaf's concept, I've compiled the following list of six servant leadership skills that represents a sampling of what servant leaders do:

- Devote themselves to serving the needs of the team
- Focus on fulfilling the needs of those whom they lead
- Develop and nurture team members to bring out the best in them
- Coach others and encourage their self-expression
- Facilitate personal growth in all whom they serve
- Listen with the goal of building a sense of community

I challenge you to step back and analyze the degree to which you have adopted these six servant leadership skills. Your ability to master them will have far-reaching implications in your personal and professional lives.

## WHO ARE THESE SERVANT LEADERS?

Although servant leaders are all around us, they are hard to spot because they are so focused on their mission—selflessly serving others. It's the teacher who is always accessible after class. The nurse who goes beyond the call of duty to care for patients. The gifted actor who accepts a supporting role in the play. The volunteer whose passion is serving the community. The star athlete who cares less about personal statistics as compared to the team's success.

Great teams, organizations, and communities have servant leaders who make their own unique contributions. A servant leader is willing to risk his or her fate in order to do what is right. It is the politician who champions an unpopular policy because it is in the best interest of the country. It is the coach who benches the star player because the team chemistry is at risk. It is the coworker who accepts full responsibility for a failed project even though many team members were involved.

While there are many servant leaders who come to mind, I suggest that former NFL star Pat Tillman belongs at the top of the list.

Born on November 6, 1976, in San Jose, California, Pat Tillman was the oldest of three sons. He excelled at football in high school and helped lead Leland High School to the Central Coast Division I football championship. Tillman's considerable talent landed him a scholarship to Arizona State University, where Tillman thrived on the field and in the classroom. As a linebacker, he helped his team achieve an undefeated season and make it to the 1997 Rose Bowl game. He won Pac-10 Defensive Player of the Year and was selected as the ASU Most Valuable Player. Tillman also earned awards for his performance as a student, winning the Clyde B. Smith Academic Award in 1996 and 1997; the Sporting News Honda Scholar-Athlete of the Year in 1997; and the 1998 Sun Angel Student Athlete of the Year.

The Arizona Cardinals selected Tillman as the 226th pick in the 1998 National Football League Draft. Tillman (relatively small for his position at 5 feet 11 inches) played the safety position in the NFL and started ten of sixteen games in his rookie season. Of interest, he turned down a five-year, $9 million contract offer from the St. Louis Rams out of loyalty to the Cardinals. *Sports Illustrated* football writer Paul Zimmerman named Tillman to his 2000 NFL All Pro Team after he finished with 155 tackles (120 solo), 1.5 sacks, 2 forced fumbles, 2 fumble recoveries, 9 pass deflections, and 1 interception for 30 yards.

Pat Tillman and his brother Kevin enlisted in the U.S. Army on May 31, 2002, eight months after the September 11 terrorist attacks. Tillman turned down a contract offer of $3.6 million over three years from the Arizona Cardinals. Kevin gave up a career in professional baseball, as he already had signed to play for the Cleveland Indians. In September they completed their basic training together. The two brothers moved through the Ranger Indoctrination Program in late 2002 and were assigned to the 2nd Ranger Battalion in Fort Lewis, Washington. After participating in the initial invasion of Operation Iraqi Freedom in September 2003, Pat Tillman entered Ranger School in Fort Benning, Georgia, and graduated on November 28, 2003. He was subsequently redeployed to Afghanistan.

Pat Tillman was very committed to his high school sweetheart, Marie Ugenti Tillman, whom he married just prior to his enlistment in the Army Rangers. He was also very close to his family and high school friends. He repeatedly mentioned in his journals during wartime service that he drew strength from and deeply valued his wife, parents, family, and closest friends.

On April 22, 2004, Pat Tillman was killed. The army initially claimed that he and his unit were attacked in an apparent ambush on a road outside the village of Sperah, about twenty-five miles southwest of Khost, near the Pakistan border. An investigation by the U.S. Army Criminal Investigation Command, however, concluded that Tillman and the Afghan militia soldier were killed by friendly fire when one ally group fired on another in confusion after nearby gunfire was mistakenly believed to be coming from enemy combatants.

On Sunday, September 19, 2004, all teams of the NFL wore a memorial decal on their helmets in honor of Pat Tillman. The Arizona Cardinals continued to wear this decal throughout the 2004 season.

The former NFL pro was asked numerous times in 2002 why he decided to put his professional football career on hold and join the U.S. military. Tillman's response resonates with the humility and selflessness we associate with a servant leader. "Sports embodied many of the qualities I deem meaningful; however, these last few years and especially after the September 11 attack, I have come to appreciate just how shallow and insignificant my role is . . . it is no longer important."

## WHAT ARE THE CHARACTERISTICS OF THE SERVANT LEADER?

After years of studying Greenleaf's original writings, Larry Spears, president and CEO of the Robert K. Greenleaf Center for Servant Leadership, extracted the following list of characteristics that servant leaders should possess:

- **Listening:** Listening intently to others, coupled with regular periods of reflection, is essential to the growth of the servant leader.

- **Empathy:** To understand and empathize with those whom you serve means to accept and recognize the emotions, thoughts, and feelings of others, as well as their unique talents and abilities.

- **Healing:** Many people have broken spirits and suffer from a variety of emotional hurts. Servant leaders recognize they have an opportunity to "help make [such] people whole."

- **Persuasion:** Rather than using positional authority or strong-arming in making decisions within an organization, servant leaders use persuasion. They seek to convince others rather than coerce compliance.

- **Conceptualization:** When you have the ability to look at a problem from a conceptual perspective, it allows you to think beyond day-to-day realities. Servant leaders have such an ability, which also allows them to help others "dream great dreams."

- **Stewardship:** This term is perhaps best defined as "managing for others." A steward is "one who directs affairs; a guardian; a manager." Servant leadership, like stewardship, assumes first and foremost a commitment to serving the needs of others.

- **Commitment to the growth of people:** Servant leaders can be deeply committed to the growth of each and every individual they serve because such leaders believe that people have intrinsic value beyond the tangible contributions they make as workers.

- **Building community:** True community is created when people are respected and valued. Servant leaders know this and thus are mindful of the importance of building community among the men and women they serve.

## LEADING RATHER THAN MANAGING

Having established the skills servant leaders exercise in the workplace and the qualities they possess and demonstrate, let's take a look at how leadership is distinguished from management. Understanding the distinction is fundamental to your preparation for the next stages of your ascent to the summit.

Although the terms "manager" and "leader" are used interchangeably, they represent very different people with diverse personalities and worldviews. By learning whether you have the characteristics of a manager or a leader, you will gain the insight and self-confidence that comes with learning more about yourself. This knowledge will have a profound impact on your personal growth and the success of your organization.

Managing is about stewardship, control, planning, organizing, resource allocation, and problem solving. It's the act of coordinating people and resources to efficiently produce goods, strategies, or services. Leading is the process of influencing others to achieve mutually agreed-upon goals for the good of the organization. It's about vision, people alignment, culture, and communication supported by the firm's mission and guiding principles. Study Figure 6.1 for further aspects of performance that distinguish managing from leading.

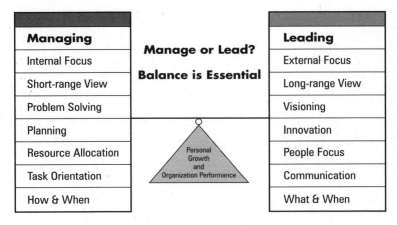

| Managing | Manage or Lead? | Leading |
|---|---|---|
| Internal Focus | | External Focus |
| Short-range View | Balance is Essential | Long-range View |
| Problem Solving | | Visioning |
| Planning | | Innovation |
| Resource Allocation | Personal Growth and Organization Performance | People Focus |
| Task Orientation | | Communication |
| How & When | | What & When |

Figure 6.1 Balancing managing and leading

To help you understand this distinction more clearly, let's take a look at the following descriptions of the two senior partners of the fictional firm Summit Ventures. Janice is the president and COO. Oscar serves as the CEO. Janice is a manager. Oscar is a leader. Their diverse skill sets offer a perfect complement for Summit Ventures. The organization continues to have unparalleled growth and profitability, in large part due to the teamwork of Oscar and Janice.

## The Manager (Janice)

Janice is an outstanding manager. She came to Summit Ventures approximately fifteen years ago to oversee the firm's P/L, operations, budgeting, reporting, human resources, stewardship, and quality assurance practices. Janice works closely with her staff in setting performance standards, meeting deadlines, and benchmarking operational efficiency and profitability. Janice is internally focused. Her gift is one of organizational metrics, a necessary and critical function for this firm. Janice often asks the question, "What operational issues need attention and what are the best means to achieve results so that my staff can best meet our client demands?" Janice is a problem solver. She is focused on goals, resources, and organizational structure. She is persistent, tough-minded, hard-working, intelligent, analytical, and tolerant. Plus, she demonstrates goodwill toward others.

## The Leader (Oscar)

Oscar started in a business development role for Summit Ventures more than twenty years ago. He transitioned into the CEO position approximately four years ago. Oscar thinks and acts quite differently from Janice. He is keenly aware of the impact of his people on the bottom line. He understands that behaviors create success. Oscar has a gift of empowering people to take ownership for their roles, responsibilities, and actions. He knows how to get his staff to respond. He is an amazing motivator and developer of talent.

Oscar is externally focused. He does not get bogged down in the details of internal process; rather, he sees his role as creating value through the design and development of innovative systems, technologies, and strategies. It is Oscar's creativity and vision that excite the staff.

## THE IMPORTANCE OF BALANCE

Great organizations have a wonderful balance between leaders and managers. Leaders are the visionaries who look ahead and plan what is to come. Managers look to the present and make sure that things get done properly. To build and grow an organization, you need leaders. And to administer one, you need managers. It is interesting to note that most leaders are not good managers. It serves leaders well to be aware of their limitations and not overstretch themselves in that role. It is easier to turn a great manager into a leader than the other way around.

The success of Summit Ventures is evidence of the importance of balance. Both Oscar and Janice understand the other's Unique Ability® and play off of one another. Figure 6.2 illustrates this ideal alignment between a leader and a manager.

**The Alignment of Leaders & Managers**

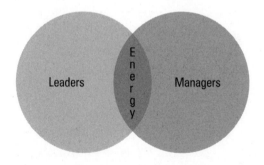

The relationship between leaders and managers is essential. The energy created by proper alignment has tremendous positive impact on personal growth and organizational achievement.

Figure 6.2: The ideal alignment between a leader and a manager

Oscar and Janice are proud to be partners, and they embrace each other's skills. Oscar appreciates Janice's management capabilities. Janice applauds Oscar's visionary talents. They each agreed to read *On Becoming a Leader* by Warren Bennis. They were so taken by the book that they wrote their own "Balanced Score Card" based on the language of Bennis himself. (Each has a copy of the document posted on the wall behind their desk.) According to Bennis's "scorecard":

The manager administers; the leader innovates.

The manager maintains; the leader develops.

The manager focuses on systems and structures; the leader focuses on people.

The manager has a short-range view; the leader has a long-range perspective.

The manager asks how and when; the leader asks what and why.

The manager has his/her eye on the bottom line; the leader has his/her eye on the horizon.

Janice has a thoughtful, consistent way of making sure that each person is accountable. Oscar is the value creator—always looking to tweak the vision of the organization. Put simply, Janice is "running a tight ship" while Oscar "inspires the crew."

On those rare occasions when the CEO and the COO get on each other's turf, the firm is paralyzed. However, the paralysis is short-lived because the staff—understanding and appreciating both individuals' strengths and weaknesses—help Oscar and Janice focus on their unique skill sets. They value the ability of Janice to bring order and stability to the corporate culture and embrace

Oscar's Unique Ability® to stir emotions, raise expectations, explore the unknown, and take the firm into unchartered waters.

Much like Summit Ventures, the success of The Addis Group testifies to the idea of having a balance between leaders and managers. Peter Unger, Bill Rhodes, and I are founding partners of the firm. We are extremely fortunate to possess leadership styles that complement one another. Peter, a CPA by training, is a gifted manager. He is precise and goal oriented and sets performance standards for all to follow. Bill is a problem solver. He has a Unique Ability® to tackle complex issues and make them simple. I am a visionary. My unique skill set is innovating and delivering strategies to enhance the customer experience.

Over the years, Peter, Bill, and I have blended together perfectly. We value each other and recognize the distinction between leading and managing.

## THE LEADERSHIP MESSAGE

Leaders inspire, motivate, and challenge those whom they serve. Their energy is contagious. However, it's becoming increasingly rare to find an inspiring and gifted leader who possesses the following five abilities:

1. **Ability to create a shared vision for the organization.** The vision must be clear, compelling, and properly articulated. The staff must buy into the leader's vision and have passion for it.

2. **Ability to build the right team.** Because leaders do not have the time and ability to execute the vision, it's

essential that the right team be in place. They must also be armed with tools to implement the vision.

3. **Ability to get out of the way**. The leader's vision creates energy, enthusiasm, and passion. On occasion, however, the vision gets diluted because the leader gets in the way of those who execute. A gifted leader knows when to get out of the way to let his or her team design, build, and execute.

4. **Ability to value people**. Great leaders understand other people's gifts and recognize their limitations. They understand the importance of recognizing the accomplishments and talents of those who support their visions. The ability to value others is an essential attribute of the successful leader.

5. **Ability to ride the wave of chaos**. Most people don't like change. They feel comfortable with the status quo. The leader's challenge is to establish a culture that embraces innovation, where the staff's energy and excitement about the future vision overshadow nervousness and anxiety.

*///////////*

Are you a manager or a leader? Your ability to understand the difference is a foundational provision of your base camp. And from there, as you ascend to the summit, you will be far better equipped to face the number of obstacles that will test your ability either to lead or to manage. You will be wise to make Greenleaf's characteristics of the servant leader and the Bennis balanced score card part of the gear you take along on your journey to the peak.

# CHAPTER 7

# Creating Your Value Proposition to Win the Battle Against Commoditization

*The greatest crime in the world is not developing your potential. When you do what you do best, you are helping not only yourself, but the world.*

**—Roger Williams**

The actor Steve McQueen starred in the 1963 movie *The Great Escape*. This thriller is based on a true story of a mass escape from a World War II German POW camp. In 1944, the Nazis, exasperated at the number of escapes from their stalags, or prison camps, built the high-security "escape proof" Stalag Luft III in Silesia, halfway between Berlin and Breslan, near the Polish border and far away from any friendly or neutral border. In it they housed their most troublesome inmates, that is, the ones who repeatedly attempted escape.

There is something demoralizing about being taken a prisoner of war. At first it stuns the mind and one is overwhelmed with a feeling of helplessness; hope is only a dim, dim shadow. The prisoner is sorely tempted to sit back quietly and cooperate with his captors. But it is the duty of any officer in the time of war, should they have the bad fortune to be taken prisoner, to do all in their power to escape. If escape is impossible, it then becomes their duty to force the enemy to employ an inordinate number of soldiers to guard them. Such was the behavior of the officers whom the Germans had corralled in the north compound of Stalag Luft III during the war.

The prison camp was grim. It held six low, drab wooden barrack huts in a patch of sand surrounded by a nine-foot-high double barbed-wire fence. Spaced about a hundred yards apart just outside the barbed wire, the "goon boxes" stood on fifteen-foot-high stilts so that searchlights could illuminate the compound without obstruction, and the guards could have unrestricted machine-gun fire. About thirty feet inside the barbed wire ran the warning wire on little posts about eighteen inches high. This was to keep prisoners away from the fence, and it certainly did. If you put your foot over the line, several bullets would follow.

With only their bare hands and the crudest of homemade tools, the prisoners built underground tunnels, forged passports, drew maps, made fake weapons, and tailored German uniforms and civilian clothes.

At this point, you might be asking what *The Great Escape* has to do with you and your business. And I would answer, *everything*. There is an enemy that is imprisoning and limiting your knowledge, wisdom, and professionalism each and every day. This enemy—known as commoditization—reduces your offerings to the lowest common denominator, the competitive bid. A stinking price!

## BRING A QUANTIFIABLE DIFFERENCE TO THE MARKET

The way to avoid the hazards of commoditization is to have a clear value proposition for both yourself and your business, an engaging statement of your worth and unique place in the market, which sets you apart from your competitors in the eyes of your customer. If you don't bring a quantifiable difference, you could end up trapped in one of the three "prisons"—the commodity prison, the perception prison, and the anxiety prison—that will prevent you from reaching your peak.

### The Commodity Prison

When the consumer sees little or no distinguishable difference between your products, services, or resources and those of your competitors, price becomes the differentiator, and you become trapped in what I call the Commodity Prison. Getting locked in the Commodity Prison is life threatening because your value proposition is reduced to a number, and it can have a negative impact on your confidence, reputation, time, and money. It also means that you have dozens, if not hundreds, of competitors who the consumer believes can deliver a similar service or product.

## The Perception Prison

The lock and key for the Perception Prison are housed in the consumer's mind and are based upon each consumer's past experiences. When people view something with a preconceived notion, they link it with prior experiences. The Perception Prison therefore alters what consumers see. And as a result, they can have preconceived ideas of the value of your products and services. Their knowledge does not allow them to open their eyes to the true value of your new offering. When concepts are viewed without understanding, the mind reaches for something that it already recognizes, a baseline of understanding on which opinions—however inaccurate—are formed.

## The Anxiety Prison

Anxiety is a reaction to stress. The Anxiety Prison represents your fear of considering alternatives to the status quo. It represents a false fear that impedes your ability to explore alternative means of delivering a product or service. Moving outside your comfort zone can cause stress, which leads to anxiety. The simplest way to escape the Anxiety Prison is to play it safe. Unfortunately, this short-term strategy will leave you caught in both the Commodity Prison and the Perception Prison as well.

///////////

So, how do you dig yourself out of these mental prisons—or, better yet, successfully avoid them in the first place? This is where your value proposition comes in.

# THE ROLE OF A VALUE PROPOSITION

How do you create value? This apparently simple question may well be the most important one you will ever be asked. Whether you are searching for a new job, launching your own business, or representing an employer, your ability to clearly articulate your value proposition will separate you from the pack, elevate your performance, and offer direction as you ascend to the summit.

Your value proposition is the reason for your professional existence. It describes how you create value for others. It makes you stand out in a crowded marketplace. Without a compelling value proposition you are ordinary and disposable—a commodity. With a distinguished value proposition you are unique and indispensable.

A value proposition statement summarizes the reason why a potential customer should buy your particular product or service, how its value exceeds that of your competition, and why it is worthy of the price they must pay. The ideal value proposition is concise and appeals to the customers' strongest decision-making drivers. It is an irresistible offer, an invitation that is so attractive that customers would be out of their minds to refuse your offer. The million-dollar question is how to make your value proposition seductive.

Most professionals do not have a value proposition in the form of a clear and concise statement that explains the tangible results their customers will receive, the unique benefits they offer that others cannot. A differentiated value proposition goes beyond functional product or service descriptions to express the results a consumer can expect to achieve. Most people attempt to sell a product or service without focusing on customer benefits or outcomes. As Jose Palomino states in his book *Value Prop—Create Powerful I³ Value Propositions to Enter and Win New Markets*, "Discovering your value starts with an honest (sometimes brutal) assessment of what assets you have to work with. The prerequisites to discovering your value are concrete ideas, available talent, industry experience and some kind of a plan for what you want to offer and to whom." (See Figure 7.1 for Palomino's definition of an I³ Value Proposition.)

## I³ Value Propositions

Your value proposition is a set of promises, based on the capabilities of credibility of the offering party, that helps prospective customers understand how an offering uniquely addresses specific problems, opportunities, and challenges.

Building a story that effectively explains the truth or substance of your offering, and tells why your target market needs it, is the essence of creating a value proposition. A strong value proposition, then, is the basis from which you can develop a well-grounded marketing message that addresses the concerns of your specific customers within a target organization.

The I³ Value Proposition describes the powerful connection your offering can have with your target customer. To develop your ability to deliver that message, you need to answer the following three questions:

1. To what extent is your product **innovative**—truly new to your target audience?
2. To what extent is your product **indispensible**—truly useful to your target buyer?
3. To what extent is your product **inspirational**—truly exciting to your target market?

—Jose Palomino, *Value Prop*

Figure 7.1 I³ Value Propositions

Let's take a look at two well-known value proposition statements. FedEx became the leading overnight courier in the world with the help of its value proposition, "When your package absolutely, positively has to get there overnight." The proposition identified that the customer did not just want fast delivery but also valued a rock-solid guarantee of urgent, on-time delivery.

The powerful value proposition of M&M's candies made customers realize that chocolate did not have to make a mess: "The milk chocolate melts in your mouth, not in your hand." This statement had an impact on both parents and children alike.

Which of the following two value proposition statements would you be most likely to respond to?

1. "We offer one-stop shopping. My company can offer you a full range of products and services to meet your every need!"

2. "After using my unique approach, one customer saw a 30 percent reduction in expenses and a 25 percent increase in traffic. Through the utilization of my system, you will realize significant impact to your bottom line."

Clearly, the more riveting statement is the one that addresses a specific customer need with tangible benefits. What could be more attention grabbing than reducing expenses and generating revenue?

In developing your value proposition, consider the following realities:

- Value cannot be created unless the customer has a business problem or issue to solve.

- Value is in the eyes of the beholder. Each customer has a different set of needs and business issues. Your value proposition should be customized to the specific needs of each customer. It is imperative that your value proposition not be about you. It is not about your products, services, or resources. It is all about the customer. Your ability to articulate how you are uniquely qualified to help the customer will distinguish you from others in the marketplace.

- A value proposition based solely on product features, functions, performance, and pricing is not sustainable. You may win in the short term, but you will lose when your competition introduces better capabilities.

- Your true value lies outside the product or service you are selling. You can create tremendous value through the intangibles brought to bear in a relationship. These intangibles include the confidence, trust, and reliance bestowed upon you as a result of the knowledge you have gained about your particular customer.

## A Real-World Value Proposition

Over the years, I have created numerous value propositions for The Addis Group and Addis Intellectual Capital to differentiate and create space from our competitors in the marketplace.

I would like to highlight one example—the Certified Risk Architect®.

The Certified Risk Architect®, or CRA, is the new breed of insurance agent: consultative, diagnostic, results oriented, and focused on managing and mitigating risk rather than selling insurance. The CRA is viewed as a trusted business advisor, not a vendor of product. The CRA's disciplined approach, planning process, and service standards differ significantly from the traditional insurance agent or broker.

The CRA has been trained to begin each engagement with a blueprint focused on the identification, evaluation, and measurement of risk: in other words, a complete enterprise, diagnostic risk management checkup. The CRA uses an audit process to develop a clear understanding of his or her client's operations, exposures, and risk profile. While the short-term objective is to evaluate risk, the long-term goal is to positively impact an organization's bottom line through the strategic elimination, reduction, and/or shifting of risk.

The CRA's passion to learn the business and its industry through a structured, consultative, and diagnostic process allows the consumer to clearly differentiate this professional from the traditional insurance agent. The process benefits the business in terms of lower premiums, better safety records, enhanced HR practices, and improvement in employee morale, absenteeism, and productivity. The Certified Risk Architect® meets Palomino's "I$^3$ Value Proposition Test": innovative, indispensable, and inspirational.

///////////

The prisoners in the *The Great Escape* made a choice to exhibit extraordinary persistence, innovation, and faith in their own purpose—and these qualities led, ultimately, to their freedom. Each of us, in our own way, must remain determined to value our special place in the market and to communicate this value clearly to set ourselves apart from others. Most of all, a clear value proposition will help you to avoid commoditization and to be noticed and appreciated for what you truly are and what you have to give.

How do you create value? Your answer to this question has profound implications in determining your future success, your ascent to peak performance.

# CHAPTER 8

# Building Your Relational Network

*The treacherous, unexplored areas of the world are not in continents
or the seas; they are in the hearts and minds of men.*

**—Allen E. Claxton**

Congratulations! You have created a solid foundation of self-confidence, servant leadership, and value proposition. To further secure your base camp before your ascent to the summit, you now need to prove yourself in the ultimate test—building deep, long-lasting relationships.

You will recall that I spoke of my grandfather, Freddie, in the introduction. Freddie's success in the restaurant business was not just about hard work. It also reflected his ability to connect with people and make others feel important and valued. He often spoke about the value of relationships built on trust and mutual respect, on generosity, not greed. Relationships, in other words, that no dollar amount could be assigned to. He must have told me ten thousand times, "The single most important ingredient to success in life is knowing how to get along with people, how to build relationships."

Relationships don't just happen. They evolve over time. Successful people in business understand that relationship building is more like farming than hunting. Quality relationships are rarely pursued and captured. Rather, exceptional relationships are rooted in rich soil consisting of a blend of mutual trust, respect, and shared values. When fully grown, these relationships produce bonds and connections that enhance both parties' opportunity to succeed.

Research indicates that 88 percent of executives view the strength of client relationships as the primary reason why the revenue goals of their companies are achieved. Mutual trust and respect are at the heart of these relationships. Mutual trust is the shared belief that one can depend upon another person. Trust grows out of confidence in another person's honesty, integrity, and desire to serve. Respect is the outgrowth of trust.

A few years ago I had a luncheon meeting with Chris Malone and Ed Wallace, managing partners of The Relational Capital Group (www.relcapgroup.com). Chris is one of the foremost branding experts in the United States. Ed is the celebrated author of the award-winning book *Business Relationships That Last*. Chris and Ed enable their clients to achieve goals through a unique five-step business relationship process. As a result of The Relational Capital Group's system, acquaintances can be turned into professional peers and, ultimately, trusted advisors.

In *Business Relationships That Last*, we learn about the Principle of Worthy Intent, Relational Capital, and Relational GPS®. Here's a brief summary of each:

**The Principle of Worthy Intent** is the inherent promise you make to keep the other person's best interests at the core of your business relationship. This speaks to your character.

**Relational Capital** is defined by Wallace as "the distinctive value created by people in a business relationship." Your ability to create relational capital with clients, prospects, and centers of influence is the most meaningful way for you to distinguish yourself.

**Relational GPS®** guides you through developing outstanding business relationships. Getting where you want to go in business is contingent on understanding your clients, prospects, and centers of influence. The *G* in the term "Relational GPS®" stands for goals—short- and long-term personal and professional objectives. The *P* stands for personal and professional causes that your client, prospect, or center of influence cares about deeply. The *S* stands for struggles, the obstacles that hold your client, prospect, or center of influence back from their goals and passions.

The three essential qualities at work in the creation of Relational Capital are credibility, integrity, and authenticity. Credibility is the quality that makes others believe in you, your words, and your actions. Credibility is the outgrowth of your professional competence. Integrity is being trustworthy in actions and character. It is the quality of having honest and truthful motivations. Authenticity is the quality of being genuine. It is about being who you are.

When worthy intent is your guiding principle, then credibility, integrity, and authenticity are easily recognized and valued by clients, prospects, and centers of influence.

People will not share their goals, passions, and struggles with you until they feel confident and comfortable in the relationship. Your credibility, integrity, and authenticity build Relational Capital and, therefore, lead to Relational GPS. Once your client, prospect, or center of influence allows you to navigate through his or her goals, passions, and struggles, you have the road map to a long-term relationship. Relational GPS also facilitates your ability to move through the sales cycle meaningfully and successfully.

Your business relationships are parked in neutral if you have little or no understanding of the other person's goals, passions, and struggles.

In *Business Relationships That Last*, Wallace says that only 24 percent of corporations formally track the relational aspects of their client and prospect interactions within their customer relationship management system. In addition, 70 percent of business professionals overestimate the quality and strength of their relationships.

When customer relationships are not benchmarked, you do not know how a customer is feeling about your value proposition. Identifying and benchmarking core relationships is an essential strategy toward your goal of building deep, long-lasting relationships.

## "ACRES OF DIAMONDS": A CAUTIONARY TALE ABOUT RELATIONAL CAPITAL

Ben Jones, a thoughtful third-generation business owner, came to work on Monday morning three years ago to learn that his five key salesmen had decided to exit his firm. They were leaving immediately to set up shop at Ben's biggest competitor, located on the other side of town.

Ben was devastated by the news, as he had invested so much in each of his five salesmen. He treated them like family and compensated them fairly. He had even gone out of his way to make sure that each one received a sizable bonus at the end of each year. In his early sixties, Ben had hired an outside consultant the year before to work with this group on a perpetuation plan. Although Ben was aware that his salesmen were frustrated about the time involved in the succession plan negotiations, he had no idea they would walk out, much less go to his biggest competitor!

A man of honor and integrity, Ben sat at his desk in denial and total disbelief. His granddad, Charlie, had started the company in 1921. His dad had been active until he passed away at the age of seventy-two, ten years earlier. The company was a family treasure that meant more to Ben than anything in the world.

Ben knew he was in deep trouble because the sales team controlled over 70 percent of the company's revenues. Although Ben had been diligent in having each person sign a business relationship agreement containing non-compete wording, his attorney had advised that the agreements would most likely not hold up if Ben's customers "sought out" the departed salesmen. Clearly, the $6,000,000 revenue business was at risk and the clock was ticking.

At ten o'clock on this fateful Monday morning, Ben called for an after-lunch staff meeting to break the news to the remaining thirty-five members of his organization. He knew he had three hours to prepare for the most important meeting of his life. He needed a strategy to keep his team calm and focused. He needed a strategy to keep the customers from a mass exodus. He also needed a plan to present to his vendors and suppliers. Most important, he knew he needed a plan to protect the organization's ninety-three-year-old brand and reputation in the community.

In planning what to say, Ben remembered a story from the classic "Acres of Diamonds" speech by Russell Conwell.

One day a wise man from the East came to the home of Ali Hafed, an ancient Persian who owned a beautiful farm. The visitor spoke about diamonds the size of his thumb. He encouraged Ali to leave his family, farm, and community to search for these rare jewels. With diamonds in hand, he could put his children upon thrones. Ali Hafed went to sleep that night a poor man—poor because he was discontented. Craving a mine of diamonds, Ali sold his farm to search for the mysterious stones. He traveled the world over, finally becoming so poor, broken, and defeated that he took his life.

A few years later, the man who purchased Ali Hafed's farm led his camel into the garden to drink. As the camel put his nose into the brook, the man saw a flash of light. He pulled a stone from the water that reflected all the hues of the rainbow. He had discovered the diamond mine of Golconda, the most magnificent mine in all history.

Instead of death in a strange land, Ali himself would have discovered the acres of diamonds had he remained at home and dug in his own garden.

Ben jumped to his feet, knowing he had the plan he needed to save his company. He was going to challenge his employees to help him build an "Acres of Diamonds" Stakeholder Intimacy and Relationship Management System. The system would have to be built immediately with a keen focus on the organization's five key stakeholders—customers, staff, vendors, suppliers, and community. Ben knew that he could not build the system by himself. He would need the buy-in and energy of his entire staff.

At one o'clock, Ben faced the thirty-five dejected and unsettled members of his firm, who had many questions. Do I have a job? Will our clients leave us? Who will develop business?

In the midst of their uncertainty, Ben told the story of Ali Hafed. He challenged his staff to look deep in their hearts to save the organization. To a person, his associates were set for the challenge. Ben appointed a team leader for each stakeholder group and asked each employee to participate on one of the Stakeholder Intimacy and Relationship Management teams. At two o'clock on Monday afternoon, the teams went their separate ways to design a Stakeholder Intimacy and Relationship Management System. They were to answer the following four questions in designing their aspect of the system:

1. Why are our stakeholders (customers, staff, vendors, suppliers, and community) so important to our organization?

2. What is each stakeholder's primary need?

3. What is the organization doing now to care for each stakeholder?

4. What strategies should the firm consider to allow each stakeholder to know how much we value them?

Little did each employee know that this exercise would change the face of the company forever. By five o'clock, each team had prepared their responses. The energy created by the "Acres of Diamonds" Stakeholder Intimacy and Relationship Management exercise was exactly what the doctor ordered. In responding to the four questions, all thirty-five members of Ben's organization had a renewed vigor as well as a passion and purpose to implement change in the company. Ben's staff believed they could keep positive momentum in the organization without the departed salesmen through an implementation plan reflecting the strategies identified in question 4.

Within days, Intimacy Action Plans were built for each of the five key stakeholders. Each plan contained a variety of services, strategies, resources, and tools to shine the diamonds.

By the end of the week, Ben's organization was prepared to introduce a ten-step intimacy and relationship management system, including service plans, quality assurance report cards, stewardship reviews, educational workshops, newsletters, e-newsletters, and a host of additional value-added services.

Additional intimacy and relationship management initiatives were also in the works, including vendor and supplier "lunch and learns," customer roundtable discussions, staff and family events, and community outreach projects.

The results were amazing. Ben's staff did not lose one customer to the departed sales staff. His customers and staff quickly came to respect the system; vendors and suppliers attended the "lunch and learns" and loved the newsletters. Customer and supplier referrals came in waves. The agency's brand and reputation in the community were preserved.

The story of Ben Jones and his dedicated staff speaks to the importance of relationships as well as a process to stay intimate with those whom you serve. In today's fast-paced business environment, intimacy is becoming a lost art. Intimacy represents a close association with and knowledge or understanding of another person.

A key component to the success of The Addis Group has been the firm's Stakeholder Intimacy and Relationship Management System, which consists of "intimate touches" throughout the year in the form of print newsletters, e-newsletters, educational workshops, service plans, stewardship reviews, golf outings, and timely gifts.

The Addis Group has benefited from the Relationship Quotient™ RQ Assessment designed by Ed Wallace. This tool will allow you to determine if key relationships are at the "Acquaintance, Professional, or Respected Advisor" level, as well as what steps you need to take to advance these relationships. The RQ Assessment takes 30 minutes to complete. It includes an action planning analysis and suggestions for advancing business relationships that will have a measurable ongoing impact on the achievement of your goals and business development plans. Specifically, the RQ Assessment will help you:

1. Identify gaps in contact information.

2. Evaluate RQ scores across contact, account, and opportunities.

3. Review business development results against relationship goals.

4. Assess the status of strategic accounts.

5. Build relationship advancement as a core competency of your daily work.

The RQ Assessment includes an overall RQ score as well as a detailed assessment report.

//////////

Whether you choose to use the RQ Assessment or another tool, it is essential that you realize that deep, long-lasting relationships will give you lift on your quest to reach your peak and elevate your customers' experience.

# CHAPTER 9

# Finding the Right Mentor

*Human potential, though not always apparent, is there*
*waiting to be discovered and invited forth.*
**—William W. Purkey**

While relationship-building skills are critical to reaching peak performance, no single relationship may be more valuable to you as you work your way toward the summit than the one you can have with a well-chosen mentor.

Your business associates, friends, relatives, the Web, industry associations, and periodicals provide you with a flow of information regarding news, business trends, and opportunities. Industry analysts, business associates, and networking contacts share their expert knowledge. But only a mentor can truly share his or her unique wisdom with you.

While maturing as an account executive at Johnson & Higgins, I had the good fortune of being introduced to Hal Real. A practicing real estate attorney with an entrepreneurial spirit, Hal possesses many skills and traits that I admire. He is creative, innovative, passionate, driven, and a servant leader. Hal is a visionary who exudes confidence in his every move.

Hal is only four years my senior, but he already possessed the business savvy and experience of a seasoned veteran when we met. I could not wait to learn from him. Our initial relationship revolved around a business transaction. I would serve in a risk management advisory capacity for The Holding Company, a private state-of-the-art safe deposit box facility that catered to the wealth of its clientele from Philadelphia's Main Line. Our relationship soon took off. Although Hal was my client, I felt comfortable sharing with him my goals and dreams as well as my struggles. Hal is an amazing listener who always guided me in the right direction. During the critical early years of my career, he was, in essence, my mentor.

Mentorship refers to a developmental relationship in which a more experienced person helps a less experienced person, referred to as a protégé. The word itself was inspired by the character Mentor in Homer's *The Odyssey*. Though the actual Mentor in the story is a somewhat ineffective old man, the goddess Athena takes on his appearance in order to guide young Telemachus in his time of difficulty.

A mentor is someone with more professional or entrepreneurial business experience than you who serves as a trusted confidant over an extended period of time. Mentors offer this service first and foremost as a way of giving back. They do it because they care about and respect you. They may do it to develop their skills as a teacher, manager, strategist, or coach. And, a true mentoring relationship works in both directions—the mentor learns about new ideas from you, just as you learn timeless wisdom from your chosen mentor.

The mentor's role is to provide an appropriate degree of challenge as well as emotional, technical, and tactical support so that you can build competence and confidence. The mentor is an information source who supports you in your decision making and problem solving with ongoing encouragement. His or her nonjudgmental approach is critical because your development hinges upon self-discovery.

A mentor must possess a special combination of traits including, but not limited to, patience, trustworthiness, listening skills, positive attitude, technical competence, brutal honesty, toughness, and a keen desire to help. Carefully evaluate prospective mentors to assess their ability and desire to serve in this valuable role. Bill Gates offers the following wisdom in this regard: "It's important to have someone you totally trust, who is totally committed, who shares your vision, yet who has a little bit different set of skills and who also acts as something of a check on you. Some of the ideas you run by him, you know he's going to say, 'Hey, wait a minute, have you thought about this or that?' The benefit of sparking off of somebody who has got that kind of brilliance is that it not only makes business more fun, but it really leads to a lot more success."

Before deciding on a mentor you feel is right for you, consider the following five guidelines:

1. **Know yourself.** Consciously think about where you are in your career and where you would like to be. Assess what type of personality you have and which personality types complement your style. Consider your strengths and weaknesses and define how a mentor might best guide you.

2. **Keep an open mind as to who this person might be.** A mentor is someone who will help you to grow in areas that are most important to you. This person is not necessarily your best friend or supervisor, a person with a high-ranking title, or even someone in the same business. It's far more important for you to look for an individual who exemplifies the traits and skills that you want to adopt.

3. **Identify where you may find a suitable mentor.** Good sources of mentors include your professional network, your management team, an industry association, online communities, and professors. You may also wish to consider people in your non-workplace communities such as retirees, local business leaders, and people associated with your hobbies.

4. **Know what you want to achieve from the relationship.** This is essential. A clear understanding of your purpose and the desired result will ensure that you find a suitable mentor. Without knowing what you wish to achieve, you will waste your time and that of the mentor. In the best of all worlds, it is not just you who will benefit from the relationship. The mentor will also see the opportunity for personal growth.

5. **Think about people who have mentored you in the past.** Whether formally or not, you have had mentors in the past. Think about people who have mentored you and the qualities that you appreciated most about them. Use these traits as barometers in determining the traits you desire in your new mentor.

It is essential in this type of relationship for you to understand that the responsibility for your growth and development belongs to you, not your mentor. It is up to you to identify personal and business objectives such as work-life balance, professional presence, career advancement, and business development. You must also be careful not to assume that your mentor will be more actively involved with you beyond the terms that you mutually agree upon. If you set unrealistic expectations, you and your mentor may be frustrated and disappointed.

Finding the right mentor is not easy. But, as one who serves as both a mentor and a protégé, I strongly recommend the journey. My mentoring experiences (on both sides of this relationship) have enhanced my personal and professional development and increased my sense of confidence and capability. As I move ahead in my career, I continually seek individuals who possess the characteristics I deem important in (and as) a mentor.

///////////

Find the right mentor, and you'll find the payoff is huge. He or she will inspire, guide, and protect you as you set off from base camp to reach for the peak.

# CHAPTER 10

# Recognizing the Importance of Your Emotional Intelligence

*One does not climb to attain enlightenment; rather
one climbs because he or she is enlightened.*

**—Zen Master Futomaki**

Successful people have many things in common, and one of the traits they share is a high degree of emotional intelligence. Just what is emotional intelligence, and why is it so important to you? In a nutshell, it represents your ability to comprehend emotions in yourself and others. It is your capacity to recognize feelings and use this knowledge to motivate, inspire, and direct. Emotional intelligence has two components:

1. Understanding and managing your own emotions.

2. Understanding and promoting positive relationships with other people.

The concept was first identified in the 1930s as "social intelligence," that is, the ability to get along with others. Psychologists continued to develop the theory through decades, and in 1995 it attained widespread acceptance with the publication of *Emotional Intelligence: Why It Can Matter More Than IQ* by Daniel Goleman, PhD.

## WHAT IS THE DIFFERENCE BETWEEN IQ AND EI?

Intelligence Quotient (IQ) and Emotional Intelligence (EI) are two separate and distinct aspects of who you are. They are completely independent of each other; you can't predict one simply by knowing the other. It is possible to have high EI with a low IQ or conversely to have a high IQ and be clueless from an EI perspective. My wife, Bobbie, often uses the expression, "Some of the smartest people do the dumbest things." How true.

Does a high IQ help drive career success and performance? Surprisingly, intelligence quotient is not correlated to achievement, as you may assume. Rather, emotional intelligence is a far more valuable predictor of success. On a pie chart of the factors that contribute to life success, experts would assign only about 20 percent to IQ. IQ is a key attribute of those who are selected into the initial pool of college students, job candidates, and similar groups, but differences in IQ are not powerful predictors of success among those who make it past the initial intelligence threshold for their career.

In professions demanding the highest level of IQ—and therefore setting the intellect bar high for participation in the field—IQ has weak predictive power. A study of Harvard grads in professional disciplines found that entry exam results (roughly equivalent to IQ) had no correlation or even a negative correlation for subsequent career success. In highly intellectual competencies such as engineering and science, brilliance is not enough to be the best. Those who attain the highest ranks demonstrate the ability to work with, persuade, and motivate others; inner discipline; flexibility; and resilience—not just brains. In other words, they have emotional intelligence.

Success in business requires more than smarts. You must be able to develop long-term relationships founded on mutual trust as well as your technical know-how. Dr. Goleman identifies five competencies that comprise EI:

1. Self-awareness: Knowing one's emotions

2. Self-regulation: Managing emotions

3. Motivation: Motivating oneself

4. Empathy: Recognizing emotions in others

5. Social skills: Handling relationships

## LEADERSHIP DEMANDS EI

Many bright people have derailed their careers because they were deficient in emotional intelligence. While they possessed the scholastic intelligence required to be successful, they failed in leadership roles as they lacked the capacity to understand how their behavior and communications styles affected their colleagues and subordinates. EI is a key building block in developing your self-awareness and self-confidence, and it is essential that you have both qualities. It is your ability to recognize how others feel that enhances the level of trust and respect in the workplace.

If you choose not to recognize the importance of EI, it will be hard for you to lead. People who are not in touch with their own emotions and the feelings of those around them often make judgment calls that are not in sync with their environment. The most critical mistake of a leader with low EI is the failure to be accessible and fully present. These actions create the perception of being aloof, disconnected, and uncaring—a recipe for disaster in a business setting.

Let's take a look at the characteristics of the best and worst bosses in the workplace:

## Best Boss (High EI)
- Supportive
- Empathetic
- Has my back
- Fair
- Authentic
- Flexible
- Inspiring
- Gives back
- Makes me feel involved

## Worst Boss (Low EI)
- Rigid
- Insincere
- Has to be right
- Judgmental
- Does not listen
- Self-absorbed
- Does not provide positive feedback

The characteristics seen in the best bosses all require a high degree of EI, while those noted on the worst bosses list reflect a decided lack of it. In addition, those who exhibit "bad boss" behaviors are not in touch with how their actions are impacting others around them.

It is interesting to note, however, that business leaders are beginning to recognize the importance of EI in hiring decisions.

MBA programs are adding personality testing and structured, scored in-person interviews to traditional selection tools, measuring such traits as empathy, motivation, and resilience. Notre Dame, Yale, Dartmouth, MIT, and other universities are attempting to recognize EI in the admissions process and to measure testing accuracy by comparing entrance scores with how students later fare in classroom and leadership activities.

## THE RISE AND FALL OF BERNIE MADOFF

Bernard Lawrence Madoff was born on April 29, 1938, in Queens, New York. His parents were Ralph and Sylvia Madoff. Ralph, the child of Polish immigrants, worked for many years as a plumber. Sylvia, the daughter of Romanian and Australian immigrants, was a housewife. Ralph and Sylvia married in 1932, at the height of the Great Depression. After struggling financially for many years, in the 1950s they became involved in finance.

After graduating from high school in 1956, Bernie headed to the University of Alabama, where he stayed for one year before transferring to Hofstra University on Long Island. In 1959 he married his high school sweetheart, Ruth, who was attending Queens College and majoring in finance. Bernie began to study at Brooklyn Law School but later quit to begin his own investment firm. Using the $5,000 he earned from his summer lifeguarding job and a side gig installing sprinkler systems, Madoff and his wife founded Bernard L. Madoff Investment Securities, LLC. With the help of his father-in-law, a retired CPA, the business attracted investors through word of mouth and amassed an impressive client list, including stars such as Steven Spielberg,

Kevin Bacon, and Kyra Sedgwick. Madoff Investment Securities grew famous for its reliable annual returns of 10 percent or more. And, by the 1980s, Bernie's firm handled up to 5 percent of the trading on the New York Stock Exchange.

As the business expanded, Bernie Madoff began employing more and more of his family members. His brother, Peter, joined the business in 1970 as the firm's chief compliance officer. Later, Bernie's sons, Andrew and Mark, also worked for the company as traders. Peter's daughter, Shana, became a rules-compliance lawyer for the trading division of her uncle's firm, and his son, Roger, joined the firm before his death in 2006.

On December 10, 2008, Bernie Madoff's life began to unravel. After an investor informed Andrew and Mark that their father planned to give out several millions of dollars in bonuses two months earlier than scheduled, they demanded to know where the money was coming from. He then admitted that a branch of his firm was actually an elaborate Ponzi scheme. Madoff's sons reported their father to federal authorities, and the next day Bernie Madoff was arrested and charged with securities fraud. He admitted to investigators that he had lost $50 billion of his investors' money, and pled guilty to eleven felony counts: security fraud, investment advisor fraud, mail fraud, wire fraud, three counts of money laundering, false statements, perjury, false filings with the United States Securities and Exchange Commission, and theft from an employee benefit plan.

On June 29, 2009, Bernard Lawrence Madoff was sentenced to 150 years in prison—the maximum possible prison sentence for the seventy-one-year-old defendant. As an armchair psychologist, I would not be surprised if the money struggles he grew up with pushed Bernie Madoff toward get-rich tactics. A more emotionally intelligent person would have absorbed the work ethic and morals of his parents in shaping the business he created. The same goes for his lack of understanding of how his sons and his clients would react to his illegal activities. Bernie Madoff—high IQ; low EI!

## EMOTIONAL INTELLIGENCE CAN BE IMPROVED

Cognitive capacities, as measured by IQ, are largely fixed. We are who we are. But the good news is that life offers us repeated opportunities to sharpen our EI as we learn to be more aware of our moods, master our emotions, and develop better relationships with others. Our sensitivity to EI may even intensify as we age.

In addition to on-the-job success, your EI strengthens personal relationships. By recognizing your emotions and handling them more effectively, you can improve your relationships with family and friends, immeasurably improving the quality of your life and reducing stress. Your answers to the following EI test will give you insight as to your own level of EI.

1. Do you develop rapport with people easily?

2. How aware are you of others' moods?

3. Are you able to admit when you are wrong?

4. Do you make decisions that are always consistent with your values?

5. Do you accept feedback from others easily?

**6.** Do you behave in a way that builds trust?

**7.** How comfortable are you delivering difficult news?

///////////

Commit yourself to improving and intensifying your level of emotional intelligence. By doing so, it will give you much-needed wisdom in your quest to reach the peak.

# On to the Summit (Focusing on the Customer Experience)

*In a sense everything that is exists to climb. All evolution is climbing towards a higher form. Climbing for life as it reaches towards the consciousness, towards the spirit. We have always honored the high places because we sense them to be the homes of gods. In the mountains there is the promise . . . something unexplainable. A higher place of awareness, a spirit that soars. So we climb . . . and in climbing there is more than a metaphor; there is a means of discovery.*

**—Rob Parker**

You have successfully elevated yourself up to and beyond the first two segments of your journey: personal readiness and presenting yourself to others. Your ability to harness your natural strengths, set goals, and build relationships is evident. It is now time to focus on the real climb ahead—the customer experience.

The next five chapters will challenge and test you. You will be required to take risks and think outside the box. You will need to find ways to differentiate yourself. If you cannot achieve this mission, you will find yourself still in the commodity, perception, or anxiety prisons.

This section of the journey is what keeps me up at night. It is my fear of not being able to stand out in a crowded marketplace that concerns me. It is for this reason that I work diligently to form emotional connections with my customers. In chapters 11 through 15, you will gain the skills to take your customer relationships to new heights.

In Elevation III, you will be required to master customer impressions, dare to be different, create and innovate, and understand the customers' purchasing decisions, as well as benchmark the customer experience.

# CHAPTER 11

# Mastering Customer Impressions

*It is only at the first encounter that a face makes
its full impression on us.*
**—Arthur Schopenhauer**

How many times have you heard the expression "You never get a second chance to make a first impression?" How many times have you said it? Do you believe it?

Initial encounters are emotionally concentrated events. You walk away from them with a first impression that is like a Polaroid picture (or, these days, a digital photo), a head-to-toe image that appears instantly and never entirely fades. An impression is an effect produced on one's intellect, feelings, or conscience. A first impression is the mark you make in the first moments of interacting with someone.

## WHAT IMPRESSION ARE YOU MAKING?

Whenever you encounter someone new, the sights and sounds around you are picked up by sense organs and the signal is passed to the brain. These signals are then compared to the memories of past experiences. The interpretations of these signals play a key role in the first impression you form.

The brain is immensely perceptive and takes into account every minor detail of a person's facial features. Three primary characteristics in particular affect the initial engagement between two people: warmth, competence, and physical attractiveness. Within seconds of the first encounter, one's brain is interpreting signals that relate to these characteristics and play the key role in forming the first impression. Warmth is best reflected by one's outlook and attitude. Competence comes across through verbal communication. And physical attractiveness is all about appearance.

The "Warmth and Competence Model" is universally accepted as how humans perceive and judge each other. According to Chris Malone, chief advisory officer of The Relational Capital Group, this model has been researched and validated across thirty-seven countries and cultures around the world and found to be an instinctive human thought process that aided survival in mankind's prehistoric era and continues to be the way we perceive people, products, and services today.

The model is as follows: In encounters with other people, you are required to assess the other person's intentions as well as his or her ability to carry out an act. You immediately ask yourself two questions: Does this person intend good? Or does this person create the opportunity for harm? People who are viewed as warm, competent, and attractive elicit positive emotions. On the other hand, people who lack those characteristics elicit negativity. Recent research has shown that warmth, competence, and attractiveness explain over 80 percent of how people perceive each other and nearly 90 percent of the strength of business relationships.

The work of Susan Fiske, Amy Cuddy, and Peter Glick, as published in the February 2007 issue of *Trends in Cognitive Sciences*, supports the Warmth and Competence Model. Their research makes it abundantly clear that warmth and competence are essential components in understanding how a person forms and acts upon first impressions. "Warmth and competence are reliably universal dimensions of social judgment across stimuli, cultures and time," state the three authors.

Appearance is the primary aspect of an individual's personality that meets the eye. An unkempt look, body odor, or bad breath tops the chart in creating a poor impression. Communication skills fall next in line. Articulation influences the first impression as it implies intelligence, educational background, and technical competence. Apart from the words you speak, your voice modulation, your pitch, and your gestures also hold significance. Wandering eyes or fidgety gestures demonstrate a lack of interest. A sloppy posture, avoiding eye contact, a shaky voice, and nervousness are prime hindrances to a positive first impression.

## THE IMPORTANCE OF BODY LANGUAGE

Edwin L. Knetzger Jr., a remarkable leader and amazing communicator, was a friend, role model, and mentor to me until his death in December 2003. He had a way of getting the best out of everyone through the manner in which he delivered his message. Though he was gifted in using the English language, it was his body language that created remarkable impact.

I first met Ed in my interview process at Johnson & Higgins in 1980. At the time, he was the managing director of Philadelphia's operations. (He assumed the presidency of the largest privately held insurance broker in the world only two years later.) I so vividly remember his handshake, the sparkle in his eye, his warm smile, and my first pat on the back. His style, grace, and charisma were gifts that were admired and appreciated by all. While Ed's accomplishments are too numerous to list in this book, his legacy is the lasting impact he had on those who worked for and with him.

Nonverbal communication is the process of sending and receiving wordless messages. Nonverbal signals have five times the impact of verbal signals. Like the spoken language, body language has words, sentences, and punctuation. Each gesture is like a single word, and each word may have several meanings. Since nonverbal communication encompasses the vast majority of one's overall message, you must understand the impact of your body language, gestures, facial expressions, posture, and movements. Body language is the outward reflection of your emotional state and condition.

The first scientific study of nonverbal communication dates back to 1872, when Charles Darwin authored *The Expression of the Emotions in Man and Animals*. He argued that all mammals show emotion in their faces. A more recent and widely referenced study was undertaken by Albert Mehrabian, PhD, who pioneered the understanding of communication in the 1960s. His research substantiated that only 7 percent of a message is verbally communicated, while 93 percent is nonverbally transmitted. Most of what we as humans communicate comes across in our appearance, body language, and the tone, speed, and inflection in our voices. Anthropologist Ray Birdwhistell, PhD, also played a key role in understanding the impact of what he called "kinesics," which encompassed facial expressions, postures, eye movements, and gestures. Birdwhistell estimated that the average person speaks words for a total of about 10 to 11 minutes a day, and the average sentence takes only 2.5 seconds. He also estimated that human beings make and recognize about 250,000 facial expressions per day. Like Mehrabian, he determined that the verbal component of a face-to-face conversation is less than 35 percent and that more than 65 percent of communication is done nonverbally.

An analysis of thousands of recorded sales interviews and negotiations in business encounters supports the findings of Mehrabian and Birdwhistell. Body language accounts for a significant percentage of the impact surrounding business negotiations. It is also interesting to note that you form your initial impression about people within a mere thirty seconds. According to Malcolm Gladwell, in *Blink: The Power of Thinking Without Thinking*, first impressions may occur much faster—instantaneously or within an astonishing two seconds.

Because nonverbal communication encompasses the vast majority of your overall message, step back and take a closer look at your body language. The "vocabulary" of this language includes, but is not limited to, your tone of voice, eye contact or lack thereof, gestures (such as open arms, crossed legs), the clearing of your throat, and so on. Even your attire—your choice of clothing, hairstyle, glasses, and accessories—has an impact on how others perceive you. Your appearance communicates a strong message.

Not only is it important for you to be aware of your own body language, it is equally important to understand what another person's body language means so that you can effectively assess and react to others. This is particularly helpful if you interact frequently with customers.

There are five key elements that can make or break your attempt at successful nonverbal business communication.

## 1. Smile and Laughter

People who laugh and smile, even when they don't feel especially happy, make their brain's left hemisphere surge with electrical activity. When you laugh, every organ in your body is affected in a positive way. As with smiling, when laughter is incorporated as a permanent part of who you are, it attracts friends, improves health, and extends life.

As a Type A personality, I tend to be extremely focused on daily business issues. Over the years, I have been told to relax, step back, and smell the roses. This does not come easily for me. I am fortunate to have a sister-in-law, Joan Walton, who knows just the right buttons to push to disarm me. She is a master needler. Understanding that I take life too seriously, Joan takes great pride in knowing how to get me to smile and laugh. Once this occurs, I am amazed how it changes my perspective.

Like it or not, judgments based on facial appearance play a

powerful role in how you treat others and how you are treated. Psychologists have found that traits such as likeability, competence, and trustworthiness are interpreted from facial expressions. Your smile is most important. When you smile, you are likely to get a warm reception. It is hard for the other person not to reciprocate.

Researchers at the University of California Medical School in San Francisco say we can pick up a smile from thirty meters away. If you wait to smile until you are shaking someone's hand, it might be too late. It's also always a good idea to smile when you make a call, regardless of whom you might be speaking with. The warmth of a smile creates a positive sound, even in your voice over the phone!

## 2. Eye Contact

Eye contact indicates interest, attention, and involvement. A person's eyes are always "talking" and providing valuable clues. Good eye contact helps your audience—whether it's an audience of one or hundreds—develop trust in you, thereby elevating you and enhancing your message. Poor eye contact does just the opposite. People rely on visual clues to help them decide whether to attend to a message or not. If they find that you are not "looking" at them when they are being spoken to, they feel uneasy. It is essential that you engage every member of the audience by looking at them. Remember that during the first encounter with anyone, your focus must be on that other person—not yourself. Make the other person the center of attention and importance and begin the interaction on the right note. Give the individual the opportunity to speak, with emphasis on being a good listener. The skills of good listening include stable eye contact and affirmative verbal clues that show that you are interested in learning more about them.

## 3. Gestures

A gesture is a non-facial body movement intended to express meaning. Gestures may be articulated with your hands, arms, feet or legs, or whole body. Gestures also include movements of the head, face, and eyes, such as winking, nodding, or rolling them. Often, gestures tell us something about a person or a situation that is not communicated verbally.

In the business setting, consumers rely heavily on your face and hands to draw conclusions about the passion and conviction you have toward your products and services.

## 4. Posture

Your posture tells a powerful nonverbal story. Positive body posture transmits a message of authority, confidence, trust, and power. Posture takes several forms:

1. The direction in which you lean your body—studies indicate that a person who displays a forward lean signifies his or her positive sentiment during the conversation.

2. The orientation of your body—stand or sit up straight (without appearing uncomfortably rigid) and avoid slouching or leaning over.

**3.** Arm and leg position—don't cross your arms and legs; keep your feet flat on the floor and your arms at your sides to maintain an open, accepting posture.

## 5. Touch

Researchers at the University of Minnesota conducted an experiment that became known as "the phone booth test." They placed a coin on the ledge of the phone booth, hid behind a tree, and waited for an unsuspecting subject to walk in and find it. When this happened, one of the researchers would approach the subject and say, "Did you see my coin in that phone booth? I need it to make another call." Only 23 percent of the subjects admitted they had found it and gave it back. In the second part of the study, the coin was again placed in the phone booth, but when the researchers approached the people who took it, they touched them slightly on the elbow—no longer than three seconds—and inquired about the coin. This time, 68 percent admitted to having the coin, looked embarrassed, and said things like, "I was looking around to try to see who owned it." The power of touch, whether it be a handshake, a slight grabbing of the elbow, a high-five, or a pat on the back, has a positive impact.

By understanding the importance of a smile and laughter, eye contact, gestures, posture, and touch, you will enhance your level of communication. Knowing the profound impact of non-verbal communication will also allow you to be more "perceptive" in business settings. Being perceptive reflects your ability to spot contradictions between someone's words and their body language. When in doubt, trust the nonverbal communication—what you see. While words can be manipulated, body language is much harder to control.

## A SPECIAL WORD ABOUT DRESS

A picture is worth a thousand words. So, the "picture" you present says much about you to the person you are meeting for the first time. Your dress sends a message about you, your skills, and your organization. While it takes but a few seconds to form a first impression, more than half of the first impression is based on appearance. You must ask yourself, "Is my appearance saying the right things to help me create a positive first impression?"

Professional dress is a critical component of you and your organization's brand. Maintaining a competitive edge requires that you and your staff sustain a consistent visual impression with those whom you serve. Dressing in a professional manner garners respect from the other person. Appropriate dress makes a good first impression. It also allows you to feel confident and poised. If you want to be taken seriously, you must dress for success.

## SIX MORE TIPS ON CREATING A POSITIVE FIRST IMPRESSION

Now that you understand the importance of creating a positive first impression, I would like to offer the following six tips:

1. **Be on time.** Someone you are meeting for the first time is not interested in your "good excuse" for running late. Arriving early is much better than arriving

late and serves as the first step in creating a positive first impression.

2. **Be positive, courteous, and attractive.** A positive attitude helps to create a good first impression. It also goes without saying that good manners and polite, attentive, and courteous behavior will enhance the manner in which you are perceived. Turn off your cell phone and give the new acquaintance 100 percent of your attention. Manners really matter!

3. **Do your homework**. Learn as much as possible about the person you are about to meet for the first time. The other person will be impressed that you took the time to learn about them. Google and LinkedIn are excellent research tools. Doing your homework demonstrates your conscientious nature.

4. **Be a good listener**. What do people enjoy more than anything in the world? Talking about themselves! That includes their goals, passions, hobbies, family, business, etc. Your listening skills will create a positive first impression and get the relationship off to a great start.

5. **Bring an agenda**. If your first encounter is a business meeting, come prepared with an agenda. The agenda demonstrates that you value the other person's time.

6. **Visualization**. Mentally rehearse your initial encounter before it takes place. See yourself smiling,

relaxed, and connecting with the other person. Visualize how a positive meeting will unfold.

///////////

So, yes, it's true that you never get a second chance to make a first impression. But now you know how to make your first impression a great one.

Your ability to create a positive first impression will allow you to be perceived as warm, competent, and attractive. This ability will also move you closer to the summit.

# CHAPTER 12

# Dare to Be Different

*If you ignore your uniqueness and try to be everything*
*for everybody, you quickly undermine what makes you different.*
**—Jack Trout**

I n today's dog-eat-dog business environment, it's essential that you develop a strategy to stand out in a crowded marketplace to separate yourself from your competition. Simply put, it's essential for you to be different!

In chapter 7 we talked about value propositions as the antidote to the problem of commoditization. I'd like to talk a bit more about this idea—specifically, the value of having a brand that differentiates you from your competition and provides a memorable experience for your customer.

Theodore Levitt, the renowned economist, Harvard Business School professor, and editor of *The Harvard Business Review*, had the following to say in his 1991 book, *Thinking About Management*: "Differentiation is one of the most important strategic and tactical activities in which individuals and companies must constantly engage. It is not discretionary. And, everything can be differentiated, even so-called commodities such as cement, copper, wheat, money, air cargo, and insurance."

Price is the enemy of differentiation. By definition, being different is worth something. Consumers are willing to pay a premium, redefine the buyer-seller relationship, erect barriers to the seller's competitors, and establish the seller as a trusted advisor, but only when a differentiated platform offers perceived value in the marketplace.

## SEATTLE'S PIKE PLACE FISH MARKET

On a trip to Seattle in 1998, John Christensen, filmmaker and CEO of ChartHouse Learning, came across a fish market called Pike Place. As he entered the fish market, he was stunned by what he saw. Fishmongers were tossing around salmon, tuna, trout, mackerel, and crabs, as well as jokes and jabs at one another. Customers were excited and laughing, too. John was taken by the electric atmosphere as well as the manner in which the fishmongers engaged and interacted with them. Often the employees of Pike Place invited customers to join the fun, complimenting them on their fish-throwing abilities and commiserating if they missed catching a flying fish.

John himself became deeply engaged in this memorable

customer experience, a differentiated, emotion-filled sales process through which garrulous hams in bright orange overalls had taken the task of selling fish and turned it into an art. The entire purchase process was choreographed, from the tentative approach of the prospect, engagement with the fishmonger, presentation of information, closing the sale, and finally tossing the fish. Seattle's Pike Place Fish Market's self-declared business goal was to become "World Famous," and they have done it!

From that initial visit, John Christensen was inspired to create the *FISH!* film, which then led to the FISH! philosophy. Today, people all around the world gain insights into differentiation, employee engagement, customer emotion, and loyalty as well as strategies to engineer the customer experience. So what's the point? A group of people turned an otherwise mundane sales process into an emotionally packed, differentiated customer experience.

## RESEARCH ON BRAND DIFFERENTIATION

Even with all of the attention paid to branding these days, more and more people are being commoditized. In other words, fewer people are able to differentiate themselves through the eyes of the customer. Brand Keys, a loyalty and engagement research consultancy, analyzed 1,847 products and services in seventy-five categories via its Customer Loyalty Engagement Index®. It found that only 21 percent of all the products and services examined had any points of differentiation that were meaningful to consumers. The vast majority had little to no differentiation through the eyes of the consumer. How tragic. Compare this to the automobile industry, where brand differentiation is high: Volvo (safety), BMW (soul-stirring driving), Toyota (reliability), Mercedes (prestige), and Ferrari (speed), to name a few.

What, exactly, is missing? A differentiated value proposition or brand (which we discussed at length in chapter 7) supported by a unique consumer experience.

In 1990, I started The Addis Group from scratch. No revenue, no carriers, no reputation. Only a $50,000 credit line and a dream of serving as an outsourced risk manager for the middle-market business segment. Knowing that I could not compete on price or product (as I had no market clout), and believing that the middle-market consumer was starving for a differentiated approach, the concept of a Risk Management Audit (RMA) was born. This diagnostic customer acquisition process was focused on empowering organizations to identify, measure, prioritize, and mitigate business risks. Instead of starting with the traditional "bidding process," The Addis Group offered an audit process three to four months after the insurance renewal. I was aware that I had to create brand differentiation in the form of a unique value proposition. Today The Addis Group is recognized as one of the premier insurance brokers and risk management consultants in the United States. A key element to our success has been our keen desire to differentiate ourselves in the marketplace through a unique customer experience.

## CUSTOMER EXPERIENCE JOURNEY

What do I mean when I use the expression "the customer experience journey"? It is the sum of all the experiences the customer has with you and your organization—the actions and results that make the customer feel important, understood, heard, and respected. Each customer interaction molds and shapes this journey. While you may take great pride in the "features and benefits" of your offerings, it is important that you assess the degree to which you are stimulating the emotions of those whom you serve. In order to accomplish this, you must deeply engage your customers' emotions in addition to—and even above—their intellect. You will hit roadblocks unless you are able to discover your customers' goals, passions, and struggles, opening the door for an intense and lasting relationship, an emotional connection that transcends price and product. (You will learn more about the importance of stimulating customer emotions in chapter 14.)

Emotional connections are essential components of the journey. Research indicates that more than 50 percent of the customer experience is subconscious, that is, how a customer feels. The sub-conscious brain is a fertile garden in which to sow positive seeds. The mind is highly selective, processing millions of pieces of information each second. Whether you realize it or not, you are impacting the subconscious in each step of the customer experience journey.

## Six Essential Steps to a Differentiated Customer Experience Journey

In designing and delivering a customer experience journey, it is important that you have a plan to engage the consumer. Emotional engagement is the foundation of the customer experience. People rationalize personal decisions first, but they make decisions based on feelings. A great experience transcends the rational attributes of a product or service (i.e., price).

I would like to suggest six essentials that underlie giving your customers an experience that is clearly differentiated.

1. **Listen to the individual customer** discuss his or her dreams, goals, passions, and aspirations. A pleasurable and memorable experience occurs when the customer has this opportunity. This tactic has been neglected by generations of well-intended professionals.

2. **Exploit the differences** between your product(s) or service(s) and your competitors'. You must be able to highlight these differences. If not, you are part of the crowd.

3. **Demonstrate the value of your offering** so the consumer can feel the impact of the key indicators.

4. **Include creativity and passion** in building customer solutions.

5. **Demonstrate your personal commitment** to ensure that the consumer achieves the outcomes proposed.

6. **Shoot for the customers' hearts** to create an emotional connection. Engagement and loyalty require an emotional connection.

////////////

Academy Award–winning costume designer Cecil Beaton said it best: "Be daring, be different, be impractical, be anything that will assert integrity of purpose, emotion, and imaginative vision against play-it-safers, the creatures of the commonplace, the slaves of the ordinary." Daring to be different is a requirement for your climb to the summit.

# CHAPTER 13

# Creativity and Innovation

*Ineffective people live day after day with unused potential. They*
*experience synergy only in small, peripheral ways in their lives.*
*But creative experiences can be produced regularly, consistently,*
*almost daily in people's lives. It requires enormous personal security,*
*openness, and a spirit of adventure.*

**—Stephen R. Covey**

On December 17, 1903, a man walked into a restaurant in Norfolk, Virginia, and announced, "There are two loony Yankees down at Kitty Hawk trying to learn to fly." Little did this man realize that this curious pair of innovators would achieve the first powered, sustained, and controlled flight of an airplane. Orville and Wilbur Wright would survive that flight and many others.

In the 1920s, the credit card was introduced for automobile owners to make the purchase of gasoline easy and efficient for them. As companies like American Express and Diners Club made it possible to purchase meals, lodging, and merchandise with the swipe of plastic, the concept of the credit card took off.

In 1968, a scientist named Spencer Silver was researching ways to make 3M's adhesive tape stronger. He failed to meet his objective, yet discovered something new—an adhesive strong enough to stick on many surfaces but which could easily be removed and reused. In 1977, Post-it Notes hit the market. The concept did not catch on immediately, as consumers could not imagine why they would need such a product. It was not until 3M decided to distribute free samples that people understood and appreciated the versatility of the little sticky notes. Once this happened, the consumers' imagination ran wild.

What do the Wright Brothers and the inventors of the credit card and Post-it Notes have in common? Creativity leading to innovation.

People who have a gift for creative innovations tend to differ from others in three ways:

1. **Expertise**. They have specialized technical knowledge in a particular discipline.

2. **Creative thinking skills**. They are flexible and imaginative as they approach obstacles and overcome them. They see problems as opportunities to explore fresh, innovative, alternative solutions.

3. **Intrinsic motivation**. They are naturally motivated.

The ability to think outside the box is an important trait of peak performers, that is, people who thrive in an environment that supports imagination, problem solving, and the creation of fresh ideas and concepts. Creative ideas emerge when preconceived assumptions are discarded and attempts at new methods that seem odd or unthinkable to others are explored.

Are you fighting commoditization in your industry? Has your business experienced ferocious price competition, leading to lower prices, lower margins, and lower profits? If so, you are not alone. Unless you offer something unique or differentiated, price will win every time. In today's fast-paced, turbulent world, it is critical that you understand the importance of imagination, originality, diversity of perspectives, and fresh ideas. These are required characteristics to reach your peak.

Creativity is the act of producing new ideas, approaches, or actions, while innovation is the process of putting ideas into action. Creativity is always the starting point for innovation. Innovation is the successful introduction of a new thing or method or a new way to look at an "old" thing. It involves acting on creative ideas to make a specific and tangible difference in the domain in which the innovation occurs. While creativity implies coming up with new ideas, innovation is bringing these ideas to life.

Innovation is the lifeblood of the peak performer. Without it, there is stagnation. With it, there is energy, excitement, differentiation, value creation, passion, and purpose. Innovation is a dynamic process of continually considering alternative means of delivering products and services, improving customer experiences, and opening new markets. Innovation is the single most essential element to assure a safe route to the summit.

Surveys of customers consistently show that they put the highest value on people who bring new ideas, who make them think, and who find creative and innovative ways to help their business. Today customers demand more depth and expertise. They expect you to teach them things they don't know.

Seth Godin, the internationally recognized best-selling author of *Purple Cow* and *The Big Moo*, puts it this way: "The only way to grow is to be remarkable. The only barrier to being remarkable is your ability to persuade your peers to make it happen. You will grow as soon as you decide to become remarkable—and do something about it." In other words, be creative and innovative.

Creativity and innovation are not easy. They require a blend of tools, resources, rules, and discipline. Think of innovation in terms of planting seeds for a vegetable garden or flowerbed. The right combination of soil, water, sunshine, and warm temperatures will determine how well the plants grow. For innovations to thrive, the conditions must be right.

## URBAN OUTFITTERS

I have had the unique opportunity to personally witness how creativity and innovation can take a concept and turn it into one of the most successful organizations in the world—Urban Outfitters.

I am the proud brother-in-law of Dick and Meg Hayne, the visionaries behind Urban Outfitters and related brands. Today Dick serves as CEO and chairman of the board. Meg is the president of Free People, a contemporary brand that caters to women in their twenties who seek fashion-forward, uniquely styled clothing.

Founded in 1970, Urban Outfitters offered product lines that evolved from "vintage, Bohemian, retro, hipster, ironically humorous, kitschy apparel" to include luxury brands and several designer collections. What has made Urban Outfitters such an amazing success? Dick and Meg have created brands that are compelling and distinct. Each brand chooses a particular customer segment, and once chosen, creates sustainable points of distinction with that segment with an emphasis on creativity.

It is the goal of Meg and Dick to offer a product assortment and an environment so compelling and distinctive that the customer feels an empathetic connection to the brand and is persuaded to buy. Simply put, Urban Outfitters creates a differentiated shopping experience, which creates an emotional bond.

Since the beginning, Urban Outfitters has hired staff members within its targeted age group and depended on their personal style to guide merchandising strategies. Staff decided on the music to be played, even bringing in their own compact discs, and department managers were made responsible for the look of their sections. It is for this reason that the stores have maintained a "counterculture" approach.

## RECIPE FOR INNOVATION

There are five essential ingredients in the recipe for innovation: innovative leadership, acceptance of failure, openness, patience, and motivation.

### Innovative Leadership

Are you an innovative leader, a fearless visionary committed to backing bold ideas? Do you thrive in an environment where you feel comfortable and confident in voicing opinions about your organization's business model? If so, you understand and appreciate the implications of creative thinking.

The peak performer encourages questioning, risk taking, openness, and a healthy attitude toward failure. He or she challenges the status quo by asking questions such as these:

- Is there a better way?
- What if I . . . ?
- What would be impacted if . . . ?
- How would the customer react to . . . ?

Many organizations—especially larger ones—have hierarchical structures that impede idea creation. The innovative leader recognizes this and responds accordingly. Innovation cannot flourish unless the barriers to creativity are removed in order to foster a culture of collaboration and the free flow of ideas.

## Acceptance of Failure

Even the most beautiful garden has weeds. To reach your peak, you must not only water and fertilize but also kill off ideas that hold no potential for future growth. The acceptance of failure is a necessary step in the process of innovation. Your willingness to be open and tolerant of failure encourages exploration of new ideas, taking risks, and being upfront about problems.

It goes without saying that failure can impact your route to the summit. It's for this reason that a checks-and-balances system is required to spot potential problems so alternative routes can be explored. Open discussion and dialogue are the best remedy to avoid costly failures. In innovative cultures, employees are encouraged to expose their ideas for early feedback and collaboration. If a creative idea does not appear to have merit, alternative routes should be explored in a patient setting before the idea is put to rest. You may assume that tremendously successful people never experience failure. Right? Wrong! Consider the following list of people who were presumed to be failures:

- Walt Disney was fired by a newspaper editor because "he lacked imagination and had no good ideas."

- Thomas Edison had teachers who said he was "too stupid to learn anything," and he was also fired from his first two jobs for not being productive enough. In his own words, Edison professed: "I have not failed. I've just found 10,000 ways that won't work."

- Albert Einstein started speaking when he was four and only learned to read at age seven. His teachers and parents thought he was intellectually challenged, slow witted, and antisocial. He was also expelled from school.

- Oprah Winfrey was demoted from her job as an on-air evening news anchor and was told she was not fit for television.

- Winston Churchill failed sixth grade and finally passed the entrance exams to the Royal Military Academy on his third try. He was defeated in every election until at last he became the United Kingdom's prime minister at age sixty-two.

- Elvis Presley had a high school teacher who gave him a C and told him he couldn't sing! That's not all: the manager of the Grand Ole Opry told him "you ain't goin' nowhere" and "you ought to go back to drivin' a truck" before Elvis was fired at one of his earliest performances.

- Sylvester Stallone was expelled from fourteen schools in eleven years. His university professors discouraged him from an acting career, and his screenplay for *Rocky* was rejected by all but one company, which would buy it only on condition that he would not act in it.

- Abraham Lincoln suffered a nervous breakdown. He failed in business twice and was also defeated in eight elections. But all that did not stop him from becoming the sixteenth president of the United States.

- Steven Spielberg was rejected by a famous film school three times. Years later he was conferred an honorary doctorate and a seat on the board of trustees at the same school for his achievements.

- Erik Weihenmayer became the first blind person to climb the world's tallest mountain when he reached the summit of Mt. Everest on May 25, 2001. He also reached the peaks of the "seven summits," making him one of approximately one hundred people who have ever climbed the highest mountain on each of the seven continents.

## Openness

FedEx has a corporate-wide initiative called "purple promise." It is each employee's commitment to making the FedEx experience remarkable. This shared mission encourages everyone at FedEx—from employees who sort and deliver packages to those who answer phones, maintain the fleet of planes, and develop new IT systems—to suggest ideas each and every day.

While innovative breakthroughs sometimes come from a single source, the vast majority of innovations draw on many contributors. Open-source innovation, the ability for a person to tap into the ingenuity of others, offers enormous potential for creative output.

Creativity flourishes in a vibrant culture that encourages people to imagine and think about possibilities, and who have the freedom to innovate. Positive cultures have open channels of communication through which staff are encouraged to bring forward new ideas so they may be captured, vetted, and prioritized. These channels include, among others, casual brainstorming sessions, strategic planning sessions, suggestion boxes, and online tools.

## Patience

The age-old adage "patience is a virtue" applies to the process of creative innovations. Patience is required if innovation is to thrive.

I mentioned creativity and innovation champion Seth Godin earlier in the chapter. In *The Big Moo*, he states: "There isn't a logical, proven, step-by-step formula you can follow.

Instead, there's a chaotic path through the woods, a path that includes side routes encompassing customer service, unconventional dedication, unparalleled leadership, and daring to dream." In some cases, innovations take time because corporate infrastructure must be tweaked. History taught us that the automobile was a plaything until highway systems were built. The telephone system didn't work until millions of miles of wires were strung. Innovative leaders demonstrate the patience to let creative ideas ripen.

## Motivation

Creative ideas come in spades when people are motivated. An uninspired employee is not likely to wrap his or her arms around a problem. On the other hand, a motivated person can't wait to find a solution to a challenging issue.

The keys to motivation in the workplace include intellectual challenge, independence, and the proper matching of talent and capabilities to a challenge. When you feel that work is meaningful, you will explore, design, and build. 3M used the practice of letting researchers spend a significant percentage of their time on projects of their own choosing. Google mastered a similar formula. Both companies noticed that giving employees ownership of the projects that were appropriate and intellectually challenging to them enhanced their motivation to do their best.

/////////////

The recipe for creating innovation is innovative leadership, acceptance of failure, openness, patience, and motivation. These five traits will expand your horizon and give you lift as you climb to the summit. Creativity and innovation offer a spirit of adventure and a renewed vigor for your business, and they move you closer to your true, peak potential.

# CHAPTER 14

# Understanding the Customer's Purchasing Decision

*Some people are headstrong. Some people are heart strong, and most people, especially sales people, don't understand that the heart is the filter for decisions. The head is attached to the price, the heart is attached to the wallet. If you jerk the heartstrings, the wallet comes popping out of the back pocket.*

**—Jeffrey Gitomer**

s the customer's purchasing decision based on logic or emotion? Let's examine the fictional medical case of Clyde.

Clyde was a brilliant business executive who was respected by all who had dealings with him. While people responded to his warm and caring nature, it was his decision-making ability that truly set him apart. Clyde was precise, systematic, and rational. He took great pride in using logic to sort through complex issues to reach conclusions, especially when it came to purchasing decisions. Clyde had an endearing expression: "Just give me the facts. There is no room for emotion in business decisions."

Last spring, Clyde was diagnosed with cancer in the right side of his brain. The doctors advised Clyde and his family that the right side controlled his creative abilities, his center for intuitive thinking. The left side, on the other hand, was his center for reading, writing, speech, language, and memory—the analytical part of the brain. By all accounts, the surgery on Clyde was a success. The tumor was removed and he was told that he would be able to resume a full and productive life. Clyde couldn't wait to get back to work.

Upon his return to the office, he was greeted with a hero's welcome. The decisive leader was back—or so people thought. While Clyde looked terrific and spoke eloquently, there was something wrong. Something was missing. Clyde's executive assistant and management team soon noticed that he was spending countless hours deciding whom to call, what project to tackle, where to eat lunch, and even which pen to use to sign his name. It was evident that Clyde had lost his ability to make decisions. Even the simplest decision seemed impossible for Clyde. He was pathologically indecisive. He had a grave condition: analysis paralysis. Clyde's remarkable business career had come to a screeching halt.

This sad story testifies to the reality that people make decisions emotionally and support them with logic. This even includes people as systematic and rational as Clyde.

Renowned neurobiological scientist Antonio Damasio studied people who suffered damage to the right side of the brain, the part where emotions are generated. Damasio concluded that while these people may seem "normal," their ability to make decisions is severely impaired. They can logically describe what they are doing but find it extremely difficult to make decisions. The research supports the assertion that emotions are essential when a person is choosing among a variety of options. An individual's decision-making process depends on his or her emotions. In fact, emotions drive 80 percent of decision making; logic drives only 20 percent.

What is logic? It is reason supported by facts. What is emotion? It is the feeling that leads us to act and react. Emotion describes the intensity with which our body and our mind respond to an event. Emotions drive us toward pleasure or away from perceived danger. Perhaps, emotions are best described as signals from the subconscious that steer the decision-making process. This is especially true when logic sees all choices as equal.

## EMOTIONS IN PURCHASING DECISIONS

The single motivator in purchasing decisions is neither data nor facts. It is emotional response. People buy when they feel comfortable, when they feel they can trust you, and when your process feels natural and reassuring. In simplistic terms, people rationalize purchasing decisions based on facts, but they make decisions based on feelings.

It is always the heart that is touched first. So, what does this mean to you and your business? Although you may take great pride in the "features and benefits" of your offerings, it is imperative that you assess the degree to which you are able to stimulate the emotions of those whom you serve. In order to accomplish this, you must deeply engage your customers' emotions in addition to and even above their intellect. The simplest strategy is to find out what keeps your customers up at night as well as what drives them. It is your discovery of their goals, passions, and struggles that opens the door for an intense and lasting relationship—an emotional connection that transcends price and product.

A range of emotions affects customers' purchasing decisions, including fear, greed, pride, envy, anger, pain, and guilt, among others. In the business of insurance, compliance, and risk management, for example, fear is a real motivator. Fear of losing something. Fear of lawsuits. Fear of injury. Fear of risk. Fear is an emotion that decidedly impacts purchasing decisions.

I have been fortunate to be recognized as an *Inc.* magazine "Entrepreneur of the Year" finalist and one of the "25 Most Innovative Insurance Brokers in America." To a large degree, the recognition reflects the impact of The Addis Group's Risk Management Audit. As mentioned in chapter 12, it is a proprietary four-step diagnostic approach focused on the identification, assessment, and mitigation of the risks facing a business. I have instituted a similar process in numerous organizations throughout the United States. I call it the Beyond Insurance Process®, and it uncovers business risks that generate emotions in customers that lead to action. I have thus learned firsthand that emotion is the driving force in the customer's purchasing decision.

Jon Picoult, the founder of Watermark Consulting and sought-after business advisor and speaker, suggests the following five-step strategy to differentiate your customer experience to evoke positive emotions that can lead to decisions in your favor:

1. **Make it effortless:** Save your clients time and frustration. They will reward you with their loyalty.

2. **Stir emotion:** Accentuate positive feelings and mitigate negative ones, creating powerful emotional cues that will make clients remember your customer experience over all others.

3. **Capitalize on cognitive science:** Remove unsettling ambiguity from your clients' lives with expectation-setting communications that give them the perception of control.

4. **Be an advocate:** Never point; always escort. Make clients feel cared for by demonstrating extraordinary ownership and accountability.

5. **Recover with style:** When the customer experience goes awry, overcorrect on the recovery. It creates a new, memorable peak to the experience that turns dissatisfied clients into raving fans.

## ENGINEERING THE CUSTOMER EXPERIENCE

Harley-Davidson, Disney, Starbucks, Urban Outfitters, and Southwest Airlines are examples of organizations that are masters of understanding the psychology of the customer. They know how to engineer the customer experience to capitalize on emotions in the decision-making process. The success of these outstanding firms lies not only in the quality and integrity of their products and services but also in the emotional connection with the customer. They go right at the heart to create intensely loyal followers. Why else would a person find pleasure by tattooing his or her body with logos making reference to Harley-Davidson?

It's interesting to note that top-notch marketing and advertising agencies use emotion-based communications to the fullest. They know that our brain consists of three separate brains: the original sensory brain, an emotional brain, and a rational brain. The emotional brain is reported to send ten times more data to the rational brain than it receives in return.

Customer loyalty to a brand is an outcome of emotion and requires more than trust and respect. Customer loyalty requires an emotional attachment. It's this component of emotional sentiment that turns the loyal customer into a social brand ambassador who proactively enhances brand equity by generating word-of-mouth recommendations. Brand loyalty, once achieved, acts as an effective barrier against competition. And it all starts with engineering the customer experience to create emotion!

## Ten Strategies to Elicit Emotion in the Purchasing Process

There are numerous strategies to elicit emotion in purchasing decisions. A suggested Top Ten list includes the following:

1. **Ask about goals, passions, and struggles.** Create the setting for the customer to talk about his or her goals, passions, and struggles.

2. **Determine the state of mind.** Do not start with your product or service. Rather, gain a grasp of the customer's state of mind. Your quickest route to an emotional connection is found in the person's feelings.

3. **Focus on benefits, not features.** A feature is an attribute of a product or service. A benefit is the way a product or service will solve customers' problems. Benefits create emotion. Features do not!

4. **Tell a story.** Plant stories in your presentation to entertain, inform, advise, warn, and educate. Stories are capable of stimulating strong emotion.

5. **Project a positive attitude.** Emotion works hand in hand with the way one thinks about an issue or situation. Your positive attitude influences emotion in purchasing decisions.

6. **Offer testimonials.** Customers want to feel reassured about their purchasing decisions. Testimonials increase credibility and comfort in the sales process. The more specific the testimonial, the more power it has for the customer.

7. **Create visuals.** Create vivid, powerful descriptions that evoke emotions in the mind of the customer. Research substantiates that the brain is wired to react to visual stimuli.

8. **Listen.** Far too often, we get so caught up in delivering our ideas that we don't hear the voice of the customer. Ask questions and listen. Getting the customer to talk about his or her issues creates emotion.

9. **Empathize.** Your capacity to identify with customers' feelings and emotions is powerful. Empathy demonstrates a true understanding of the emotional state of the consumer.

10. **Present a future vision**. A vision is a motivating view of the future. It creates pride. It gives direction. Emotion is created by taking the customer to a future place and time and looking back. Future visions are filled with anticipation.

/////////

Your understanding of, and appreciation for, the importance of eliciting emotions in customers' purchasing decisions will give you clarity as you finish your ascent to the summit.

# CHAPTER 15

# Benchmarking the Customer Experience

*Your customers are your best advisors. They'll tell you what you are doing right, what you're doing wrong and what it is they want you to change, if anything. But you have to ask them first.*
**—Seth Godin**

Can you define customer loyalty? Can you measure it? Can you manage it? In today's challenging marketplace and unsettled business environment, it's essential that you develop the capacity to define, measure, and manage customer loyalty. It is not enough to understand your retention and growth indicators. You must dig deeper to understand why customers return, why they defect, why they buy, and what they say about you.

## THE LOYALTY EFFECT

Loyalty is commonly defined as faithfulness or devotion. Richard L. Oliver, the renowned consumer scientist and Vanderbilt University professor, referred to customer loyalty as "a deeply held commitment to re-buy or re-patronize a preferred product or service consistently in the future despite situational influences and marketing efforts having the potential to cause switching behavior." The loyalty effect is created when the consumer becomes an advocate and evangelist of a product or service. The impact of customer loyalty includes, but is not limited to, repeat purchases, brand loyalty, and positive word of mouth.

Loyalty is the key to profitable growth. Fred Reichheld, director emeritus at Bain & Company and best-selling author of *The Loyalty Effect*, *Loyalty Rules*, and *The Ultimate Question*, has documented research that reveals a 25 percent to 100 percent increase in profits from just a 5 percent increase in customer retention. Companies with the highest customer loyalty typically grow at more than double the rate of their competitors.

Customer loyalty is not a choice any longer. It is the only way to build a sustainable competitive advantage. Easy? No way. It requires a dedication to and focus on the delivery of a customer experience that transcends price and product. At the core is an experience with the customer that is so tight it wards off competition and entices word-of-mouth referrals.

## LOYALTY AND THE CUSTOMER EXPERIENCE

As mentioned in chapter 12, the customer experience journey is the sum of all experiences a customer has with an organization.

It is the single most important determining factor of loyalty. Building a memorable customer experience involves strategy, discipline, technology, relationship management, branding, leadership, and commitment all wrapped in a process to engage, surprise, and delight. You can be sure that each and every one of the world's most admired companies—Apple, Google, Disney, Walmart, Southwest Airlines, BMW, and Nordstrom, among many others—spend countless hours on how best to deliver a unique customer experience.

Customer loyalty can never be taken for granted. High-performance organizations are always tweaking, tinkering, and in some cases, reinventing themselves. Their goal is crystal clear—to deliver a remarkable experience.

To expand upon the Seth Godin statement about being remarkable that I quoted in chapter 13, he continued: "You will grow as soon as you become remarkable—and do something about it. But you must know that remarkable isn't up to you. Remarkable is in the eyes of the consumer." Anticipating the needs and wants of the customer is rule number one in building the customer experience.

## LIFETIME VALUE OF A CUSTOMER

Recognizing the lifetime value of a customer, it is imperative that you have a process in place to benchmark customer intimacy, appreciation, and loyalty. In marketing terms, the lifetime value of a customer represents the net present value of the cash flows attributed to the relationship.

It is shortsighted to view the value of the relationship in terms of the revenue derived from the initial engagement. Rather, the following factors must be considered:

- Repeat purchases over the lifetime of the relationship;
- Cross-purchasing of additional products and services;
- Price premium due to the appreciation for the experience;
- Positive word of mouth in terms of referrals;
- Appreciation and enjoyment when interacting with staff.

Many growth-oriented firms use acquisitions, aggressive pricing strategies, marketing campaigns, and sales blitzes to improve performance. While these strategies give the organization a short-term boost, they are not long-term solutions. Customer engagement and loyalty is the most solid plan. Real growth occurs because there is a "love affair" between an organization and its customers, when the customer can't wait to sing the company's praises to friends and colleagues.

Let's use an example. ABC Company becomes a new customer, bringing revenues of $10,000 for its initial engagement with your firm. Because of your organization's customer management relationship system (i.e., loyalty effect), ABC quickly becomes a "raving fan." ABC is an advocate because all expectations have been met or exceeded. The Lifetime Value Profitability Chart is shown in Figure 15.1:

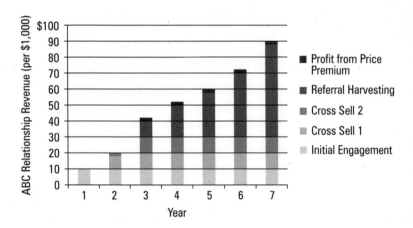

Figure 15.1: The Lifetime Value Profitability Chart

Over the course of the relationship, the following occurs:

- ABC continues its engagement on its initial product line yet becomes less price sensitive;

- ABC is pleased to expand its relationship with you through cross-sell initiatives because all its expectations have been met or exceeded;

- ABC becomes an advocate and a key referral source;

- ABC is willing to pay a premium for your experience because the relationship is of such great value to it.

In the case of ABC, the net present value of its relationship is $350,000 over the seven-year term. For a $10,000 initial deposit, what a return!

## THE ULTIMATE QUESTION

In the early 1980s, Reichheld and his colleagues at Bain began investigating the connection between loyalty and growth. The research confirmed that businesses cannot prosper without customer loyalty. Yet there was no practical metric for relationship loyalty. Companies lacked a system for gauging the percentage of their customer relationships that were growing stronger and the percentage that were growing weaker. Without the ability to gauge what people were thinking and feeling, corporate managers naturally focused on how much those customers were spending, a number that was easily measurable.

Reichheld and his team came up with twenty survey questions. Sample questions included "How likely are you to continue buying Company X's products or services?" and "How would you rate the overall quality of the products and services provided by Company X?" The goal was to find the one question—the Ultimate Question—that showed the strongest correlation with repeat purchases and referrals.

To the surprise of Reichheld, the one question—the Ultimate Question—that captured the essence of the research was "How likely is it that you would recommend Company X to a friend or colleague?" Reflecting on his findings, Reichheld and his Bain colleagues realized that this question made perfect sense because two conditions must be satisfied before a consumer makes a personal referral:

1. They must believe that you offer superior value in terms of price, features, quality, functionality, ease of use, and other practical factors.

2. They must believe that you know and understand them, value them, listen to them, and share their principles.

Today this simple question is used by many of the most admired companies in the world through a metric that produces the Net Promoter® Score (NPS). (See Figure 15.2.)

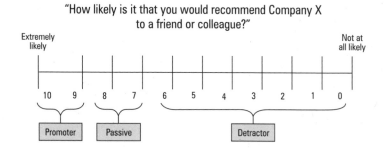

Figure 15.2: The Net Promoter Score.

The Net Promoter® Score divides your customers into three categories:

1. **Promoters:** Loyal enthusiasts who keep buying from you and urge their friends to do the same.

2. **Passive:** Satisfied but unenthusiastic customers who can be easily wooed by the competition.

3. **Detractors:** Unhappy customers who feel trapped in a bad relationship.

The formula for the Net Promoter® Score is the percentage

of customers who are Detractors (D) subtracted from the percentage who are Promoters (P). P - D = NPS.

How do legendary companies like Amazon.com, eBay, Costco, and Vanguard stack up? They operate at an NPS between 50 and 80 percent. But the average firm sputters along at an NPS of only 5 percent to 10 percent. Many firms—and some entire industries—have negative Net Promoter® Scores. To learn more about NPS, go to www.netpromoter.com.

////////////

Your ability to implement a customer relationship management system will have a significant impact on you. The loyalty effect is proven to be the most impactful strategy to achieve growth and profitability. It is your loyal and engaged customers who will guide you to the summit. Can you define, measure, or manage customer loyalty? You bet!

# The Final Ascent
# (Discovering Your Inner Strengths)

*But risks must be taken because the greatest hazard in life is to risk nothing. The person who risks nothing, does nothing, has nothing, is nothing. He may avoid suffering and sorrow, but he cannot learn, feel, change, grow, or live. Chained by his servitude he is a slave who has forfeited all freedom. Only a person who risks is free. The pessimist complains about the wind; the optimist expects it to change; and the realist adjusts the sails.*

**—William Arthur Ward**

The final ascent will push you to the limits. This last part of the climb will test your desire to be a peak performer. Your focus on the customer experience braced by confidence, servant leadership, value proposition, and relational capital will give you the motivation to push ahead. In the final ascent, you will discover your inner strengths, one of which is your ability to move past rejection.

# CHAPTER 16

# Using Rejection to Take You to the Next Level

*Continuous effort—not strength or intelligence—*
*is the key to unlocking our potential.*
**—Winston Churchill**

How well do you handle rejection? Do you brush it aside? Or does the failure to connect deflate your self-image and/or confidence? Research suggests that the vast majority of people struggle with rejection. Learning how to overcome the ill effects of rejection is an essential survival skill.

If you were able to go back in time and identify negative scenarios that influenced your moods, I bet that rejection would be at the top of the list. A significant percentage of events that impact self-esteem and confidence is related to the feeling that the other person does not value the relationship as much as you do. We experience disappointment when we fail to connect because the "drive to bond" lies deep in our DNA. It is often rejection that triggers emotions and sends self-esteem into a tailspin, especially if there is emotional investment. Self-esteem reflects an overall evaluation or appraisal of your own worth, a barometer of your standing with others. Self-esteem rises with acceptance ("Congratulations, you earned my account") and plummets with rejection ("We are moving our relationship to someone else").

## SOCIAL SELF-ESTEEM

Social self-esteem acts like radar, scanning the environment for signs of approval or disapproval. Most people fall into one of two camps: They assume that they are doing everything right and it is the rest of the world that has a problem. Or, they internalize rejection as a function of their personal shortcomings. For those who focus on their inadequacies, a blip on the meter often causes a drop in perceived self-worth. Duke University psychologist Mark Leary comments that "Nature designed people to be vigilant about rejection because for most of history we depended upon small groups of people. Getting shut out compromised survival."

Numerous psychologists agree with Leary and theorize that the pain of being rejected has evolved because of the importance of social bonds for survival. UCLA professor Matthew Lieberman suggests that "Going back 50,000 years, social distance from a group could lead to death and it still does for most mammals." As the need for social connection is deeply rooted, exclusion from others often has an immediate and long-lasting impact.

Our fragmented, mobile society has weakened the strength

of our social bonds. "Today, we are less secure," states Leary. Even two hundred years ago, people were part of a small clan. They lived their entire lives in the same town. Each and every day they interacted with a tight group of people. Today we often have to reintegrate ourselves into new social networks. The sheer number of strangers with whom we interact on a daily basis creates more opportunities for rejection. It is this increased general sense of uncertainty that makes us more vulnerable to rejection, leading to lower self-esteem and confidence.

## REJECTION SENSITIVITY

Rejection sensitivity, a condition linked to depression, is on the rise. It is rejection sensitivity that makes you cautious and in some cases unwilling to take social risks. Those who are on the high end of the rejection sensitivity scale pay a steep price because they rarely venture beyond their immediate social network. When they do, they suffer anxiety and fear. Although their pain is borne privately, it has repercussions in the manner in which they move about life.

While physical pain is understood, most people believe that social pain is in one's head. Rationally, shouldn't we be able to convince ourselves that rejection doesn't matter? Professor Lieberman's research indicates that physical and social pain may be more similar than we think, as rejection in our brain is much like a physical ailment.

There is no question that I score high on the rejection sensitivity scale. It is for this reason that I work hard to put myself in positions where rejection is not an option. This includes, but is not limited to, prospective client meetings and social situations. As a psychology major at Princeton University, I studied rejection as part of the theory of learned helplessness, the perceived absence of control of the outcome of situations. When one feels helpless, he or she becomes anxious and loses confidence and motivation. When a person fails to respond, even if there are opportunities to gain positive rewards, he or she is seen as being "helpless."

Typically, people who suffer from learned helplessness fear rejection. They have encountered the pain of failing to connect and now believe they are incapable of improving their performance. It's this erroneous fear of rejection that hinders their personal and professional progress. History reminds us that countless people have pushed through rejection to become icons, such as Colonel Sanders. Colonel Sanders of Kentucky Fried Chicken received over a thousand rejections before anyone would buy into his concept. Rejection is inevitable. You just have to keep saying to yourself, "Some will, some won't, so what!"

## USING REJECTION AS A MOTIVATOR TO TAKE YOU TO THE PEAK

Peak performers have a positive attitude toward rejection. They use rejection as a motivator, a signal that indicates it may be time to tweak their performance. They ask questions such as, "What might I do differently?" or "How can I better present my value proposition?" Before moving on to the next opportunity, they use rejection to help them change the outcome of future opportunities. If you encounter a few rejections, do not be alarmed. This is natural. Yet, a consistent pattern of rejections suggests that you need to step back and study the manner in which you are delivering your product, services, and resources. It may be that a simple tweak of your process, packaging, or positioning will create instant results.

Here are five ways to use rejection as a motivator to take you to the next level:

**Step 1:** Don't take it personally. The prospect or client is not rejecting you. Rather, they are rejecting your offering.

**Step 2:** Know when to cut your losses. Decide in advance how much time and effort you will put into the acquisition of a particular prospect. Use a "Criteria Filter" to screen out price shoppers.

**Step 3:** Rely on your support system. When you are confronted with rejection, your ego is damaged. It helps to open up to others to get your hurt feelings and frustrations off your chest. A support system enables you to heal the wound by offering encouragement, guidance, and counsel. Members of your support system can also offer constructive feedback.

**Step 4:** Maintain your focus on control. Focus on the controllable outcomes. Do not lose energy and confidence by dwelling on uncontrollable forces that influence the buying decision.

**Step 5:** Keep a positive attitude. Use your failure to connect with a prospective customer as a learning experience, an opportunity to find out what you might do differently in each phase of your business development and client service process. Every "no" you hear brings you that much closer to the next "yes."

/////////////

When next you are faced with rejection, please consider this excerpt from the speech Theodore Roosevelt delivered in Paris on April 23, 1910:

> The credit belongs to the man who is actually in the arena, whose face is marred by dust and sweat and blood; who strives valiantly; who errs, comes up short again and again, because there is no effort without error and shortcoming; but who does actually strive to do the deeds; who knows great enthusiasms, the great devotions; who spends himself in a worthy cause; who at the best knows in the end the triumph of high achievement and who at the worst, if he fails, at least fails while daring greatly, so that his place shall never be with those cold and timid souls who neither know victory nor defeat.

I have Theodore Roosevelt's quotation posted on the wall behind my desk and on a card in my wallet. The words serve as a reminder that my barometer of success need not be measured in fame or fortune; rather, success may be measured in my dedication to a worthy cause. In your journey to the summit, you will experience slippery slopes, headwinds, and poor visibility. There will be moments when you question your climb. It will be your ability to move past rejection that will allow you to realize your full potential.

# CHAPTER 17

# Discovering Your Inner Game

*The will to win, the desire to succeed, the urge to
reach your full potential . . . these are the keys that will
unlock the door to personal excellence.*
**—Eddie Robinson**

My senior thesis in college was titled "An Analysis of Athletes in Pressure Situations." As a psychology major and student athlete at Princeton, I was curious to understand the mental aspects that create success or failure in sports and in life—the "inner game," if you will. I have come to learn that the emotions and lessons learned in sports have tremendous applicability to our daily work in our chosen fields. As you dig deep inside your heart and soul to gain energy for the final ascent, consider the following attributes, attitudes, and determinations.

## MENTAL TOUGHNESS

An essential ingredient in achieving success in sports and in life is your ability to focus on a task and not let negative thoughts intrude. A key strategy to confront mental toughness is your ability to handle pressure. Pressure can be both a positive and a negative force. Pressure affects each person differently. Confronted with pressure, people may weigh the benefits of success and the pains of failure at the same time. Peak performers often do not feel pressure. They are so immersed in the game that they do not have time to understand the magnitude of the moment. Mentally tough professionals know how to stay focused and, most important, how to deal with adversity. They understand the importance of controlling their emotions. It is this inner strength that allows them to achieve peak performance even in the most pressure-packed situations.

Peak performers have warrior mentalities. They stand tall even in the most difficult of circumstances. They understand the importance of demonstrating confidence and poise at all times.

In your ascent to the summit, you will be required to persevere through difficult circumstances and emerge without losing confidence. It will be your unshakable belief in your ability and motivation to succeed that will allow you to develop the psychological edge to reach the summit, your peak potential.

## SELF-IMAGE

Your positive self-image is essential to success. If you do not feel good about yourself, your performance will suffer. A negative self-image can hinder the performance of even the most gifted professional. Athletes must learn how to deal with anxiety, fear, and distractions; for them, positive self-image is an essential ingredient to achieve success.

A positive self-image is a requirement to summit the peak. When you feel good about yourself, your self-confidence grows and performance skyrockets.

## COMMITMENT

Amazing performances don't just happen. They are the result of your dedication, determination, and sacrifice. Commitment starts in the athlete's heart and soul. Every athlete faces numerous obstacles and opposition. Commitment gives you inspiration to carry forward even when confronted with tremendous challenge and turbulence. In life, as in sports, there is no substitute for commitment.

Your untapped potential will never be realized without devotion and dedication to self-improvement. Your journey to the peak will require hard work, focus, and emotional engagement.

## GOAL SETTING

Athletes are experts at setting goals. At a young age, they learn that goals are essential to their development. As mentioned in chapter 3, goal achievement brings rewards. Success cannot be measured or achieved without setting specific goals. You understand that setting goals is an art. Goals set too high or too low can impede progress.

Goals improve performance. Your ascent to the summit will

require you to master the art of goal setting. Your goals are a form of motivation that sets the standard for self-satisfaction and performance.

## FEAR OF FAILURE

Fear creates tension, doubt, and panic. Fear of failure impacts your ability to achieve performance at the highest level. It increases muscle tension as well as your heart and respiratory rates. Fear of failure causes narrowed perception and attention as well as diminished cognitive flexibility. Fear of failure is the toughest opponent you will ever face. When you are not afraid to fail, your chances of success improve dramatically.

Playing it safe will not allow you to realize your potential. To reach your peak, you will be required to be bold and decisive. If you never dare to fail, your success will have a low ceiling.

## MOTIVATION

Your desire to succeed must be stronger than your fear of failure. Motivation is the key. Motivation starts with a sense of purpose. It is rooted within one's heart and soul. Motivation is a combination of desire and energy directed at achieving a goal. People find motivation in different ways. For some it's a mission to be accomplished. For others it's fulfilling a lifelong dream. Often this dream turns into a burning desire to reach a specific goal. Playing with purpose and passion comes easily for athletes who are motivated by their desire to achieve.

In your quest to discover your true potential, motivation is essential. It will be your desire and motivation that activate you to push on when confronted with difficult challenges.

## DRIVE

Drive is a common denominator found in nearly all peak performers. Drive is so important and so powerful that it often pushes less talented individuals beyond those people who have been born with higher skills but lack a burning desire to succeed. Drive is often the starting point of motivation.

Why is drive so important? Because it requires intense self-motivation in the face of rejection, and because your business practice exerts grueling and constant pressure on self-esteem. Only people who love to compete have supreme confidence in themselves. They are willing to laugh in the face of rejection and have the constitution to thrive in today's competitive business environment.

While your relationship skills, value proposition, emotional intelligence, and passion are important, these traits are not sufficient without drive. After studying over eighty years of research in the sales sector, Richard Abraham, speaker, writer, and consultant to many Fortune 500 companies, and Christopher Croner, PhD, a principal with Sales Drive, uncovered the following three traits that make up drive: need for achievement, competitiveness, and optimism.

In your final steps to the summit, you will need to dig deep inside yourself to capture the willpower necessary to motivate you to realize your goals and dreams.

## VISUALIZATION

The power of visualization and mental rehearsal has been universally viewed as an effective means to improve performance. Imagery, or visualization, is viewed as one of the most important mental skills for winning the mind game in sports. It allows athletes to see themselves performing "in the zone." When athletes are in the zone, everything around them seems to slow down. They are able to see the game with clarity and understanding.

Great athletes roll their mental camera before performances. They understand the benefits of creating visible and clear images. Your ability to see yourself succeeding breeds confidence. Confidence is the result of preparation. Preparation begins with a mental game plan.

As mentioned in chapter 3, visualization is a mental technique that uses imagination to make dreams and goals come true. By visualizing your goals as having already been accomplished, you will feel great exhilaration when the summit actually becomes your reality.

## POSITIVE ATTITUDES

Attitudes influence how you act and feel. Attitude is a choice that has a profound impact on performance. Positive attitude gives you a competitive edge; negative attitude impairs peak performance, especially in team-oriented contests. It has been said that 10 percent of a performance is what happens to an athlete and 90 percent is how the athlete chooses to react to it.

Golfer Arnold Palmer kept a copy of the following poem by Walter D. Wintle in his locker:

*If you think you are beaten, you are*
*If you think you dare not, you don't,*
*If you like to win, but you think you can't*
*It is almost certain you won't.*

*If you think you'll lose, you're lost*
*For out in the world we find,*
*Success begins with a fellow's will*
*It's all in the state of mind.*

*If you think you are outclassed, you are*
*You've got to think high to rise,*
*You've got to be sure of yourself before*
*You can ever win a prize.*

*Life's battles don't always go*
*To the stronger or faster man,*
*But soon or late the man who wins*
*Is the man* **WHO THINKS HE CAN!**

In a team setting, teammates often mirror your attitude. Your positive attitude inspires others to succeed. A negative attitude brings a team down. A positive attitude is the power that will drive you and your team to success. It is the special ingredient of those performers who have reached the peak in their personal and professional lives.

## SELF-DISCIPLINE

Great performers are highly disciplined. Hall of Fame athletes often look back on their careers and understand that an essential ingredient to their success was self-discipline. Self-discipline begins with setting priorities, designing one's lifestyle based on achieving goals. In developing a lifestyle of discipline, the athlete learns how to eliminate excuses. Disciplined athletes are highly focused on goals and specific results. They are not focused on the challenge of their athletic performance; rather, they look to the rewards of achievement.

//////////

Because your personal and business lives require character, commitment, mental toughness, motivation, and positive attitude, an understanding of the inner game will help you with your emotions, actions, and attitudes as you take your last steps to reach the summit.

While each of the ten attributes described in this chapter are essential to reach your peak, I suggest that self-discipline is the most important. Self-discipline will have a profound impact on maximizing your potential to realize peak performance.

# Your Decision to Climb

*Deciding to go is the first step on the journey to becoming a Category of One. Unfortunately, it's also the step usually not taken. Most individuals and companies never decide to go. They never make the decision to become extraordinary. The decision they make is to talk about becoming extraordinary or to have meetings about becoming extraordinary or to write mission statements about becoming extraordinary. But they never "decide to go," that is, make the commitment that takes hold, becomes real, and creates a new level of success.*

—*Joe Calloway*

The first time I was asked to speak professionally was in 1998. I was to address a group of about eighty professionals at the St. Paul Insurance Company Top Brass Conference held in Tucson, Arizona. I prepared as though my life depended on it and delivered a two-hour program with every ounce of my heart and soul. I presented my card as never before. When I completed the program, eighty strangers stood on their feet to congratulate me on my performance. I had never experienced anything quite like that before. The applause hit a warm spot—I was hooked.

I returned to my office and tried to forget about the program in Tucson. I went back to building my award-winning company, The Addis Group. However, the feeling from that day in Tucson did not disappear. The urge to teach, coach, and mentor was spreading inside of me like wildfire. Because The Addis Group demanded my full attention, I suppressed my hidden desire.

All that changed on an October evening in 2001. It was on that night that my father-in-law, Bill Annesley, was recognized by those whom he had trained at Wills Eye Hospital in Philadelphia. A humble man who grew up in the City of Brotherly Love's Kensington area (a tough neighborhood), Bill went on to have an astonishing career as an ophthalmologist. He was world-renowned for his technical skills as well as his contribution to his profession. Although he was juggling many responsibilities as the chief of the Wills Eye Hospital Retina Department, he always took the time to guide those in his profession and care for his family. I often recall him speaking proudly of the success of those whom he had coached, trained, and mentored.

On that October evening, Bill was the guest of honor at a surprise party at the Pennsylvania Academy of Fine Arts to which more than a hundred ophthalmologists from all over the world—Japan, South Africa, England, Denmark, among others—came to salute him, to thank him for the manner in which he touched them, to let him know how much he had given them, and to express deep appreciation and gratitude. Bill Annesley was much more than a talented ophthalmologist. Much more than a loving husband, father, and grandfather. He was a difference maker—the beloved coach, trainer, and mentor.

For three years leading up to that evening, I had been thinking about mentoring others. Yet I had not made the commitment to take action. Things changed that evening. Like Bill, I wanted to be a difference maker. To follow in his footsteps. To have my kids and grandkids see me the way I saw him, a person giving of himself to others in such a selfless way. That night I decided to go—that is, commit to myself that I would one day be a talented business coach and mentor.

You can't reach your peak until you decide to go. Is there a better time than now?

> *You cannot stay on the summit forever; you have to come down again. So why bother in the first place? Just this: What is above knows what is below, but what is below does not know what is above. One climbs, one sees. One descends, one sees no longer, but one has seen. There is an art of conducting oneself in the lower regions by the memory of what one saw higher up. When one can no longer see, one can at least still know.*
>
> **—René Daumal**

# About the Author

*Inc.* magazine named Scott Addis an "Entrepreneur of the Year" finalist, and The National Alliance for Insurance Education & Research honored him as one of the "25 Most Innovative Agents in America." In addition to serving as president and CEO of The Addis Group and Addis Intellectual Capital, he is founder of the Beyond Insurance® Global Network and innovator of the Certified Risk Architect® and Reach Your Peak™ programs. Scott reached a new peak a decade ago by pursuing the additional role of executive coach and speaker.

Scott started his award-winning company, The Addis Group, in 1990—from scratch: No carriers. No revenue. Only a $50,000 credit line and a vision of providing elite risk management services to the middle-market business segment. It has evolved into a juggernaut in the industry, with more than 1,700 clients, total premiums in excess of $180,000,000, and revenues of over $16,000,000. The firm has been listed three times as one of the "Philadelphia 100," the fastest-growing firms in the region, and has been named one of the best places to work in Pennsylvania.

Prior to starting the Addis Group in 1990, Scott served as vice president and senior account manager for Johnson & Higgins (now Marsh USA). While there, he handled insurance placement for some of Philadelphia's most prestigious companies and institutions, including Comcast Corp., Aqua America, Temple University, University of Pennsylvania, Lukens Steel, and U.S. Healthcare. Scott also played a key role in the growth of Johnson & Higgins's middle-market division.

Scott has served as a member of the American Institute for Chartered Property Casualty Underwriter's Advisory Committee. He currently sits on the Educational Advisory Board for *Rough Notes®* magazine.

A resident of Bryn Mawr, Pennsylvania, with his wife, Bobbie, Scott is active in community affairs, and he has been recognized by the *Philadelphia Business Journal* as one of the region's most influential business professionals in its "Book of Leaders."

He is the proud father of three sons—Andrew, Jeff, and Will—as well as the proud father-in-law of Lauren and Erin and grandfather of beautiful Fern.

# Index